THE CITY OF LONDON

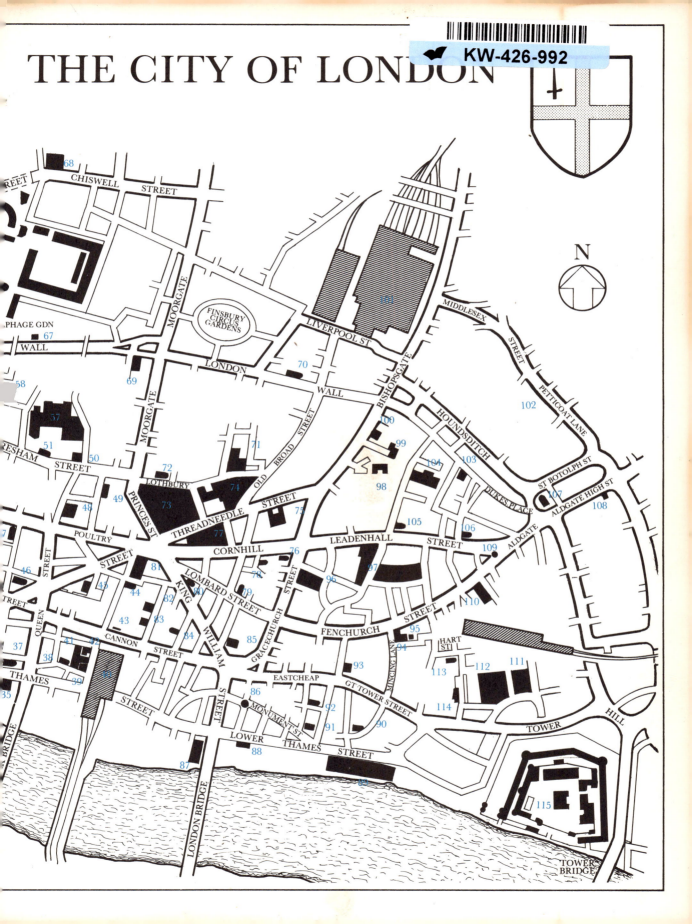

THE CITY OF LONDON

THE HISTORIC SQUARE MILE

Text by
ANGELA FIDDES

With photographs by
ERNEST FRANKL

THE PEVENSEY PRESS

Cambridge England

Contents

Published by The Pevensey Press, 6 De Freville Avenue, Cambridge CB4 1HR, UK

Photographs: Ernest Frankl, except 35: Nicholas Servian, Woodmansterne Ltd; 36: reproduced by courtesy of the Museum of London; 52: reproduced by courtesy of the Stock Exchange; 64: Howard Moore, Woodmansterne Ltd

Map: Carmen Frankl

The assistance of Mr Gerry Curry and Miss Beryl Footman is gratefully acknowledged

Edited by Michael Hall and Ruth Smith

Design by Kate Hughes-Stanton; design and production in association with Book Production Consultants, Cambridge

© Ernest Frankl and The Pevensey Press, 1984
First published 1984

ISBN 0 907115 17 9 (hard covers); 0 907115 18 7 (paperback)

Typesetting in Baskerville by Westholme Graphics Ltd

Printed in Hong Kong

Front cover: St Paul's Cathedral from the south-east. The cross which surmounts Sir Christopher Wren's masterpiece (built between 1675 and 1711) is 365 feet (110 metres) above the ground. The serenely beautiful dome remains the most memorable feature of the City's skyline.

Back cover: Goldsmiths' Hall, Foster Lane (1835), designed by Philip Hardwick, is probably the most impressive hall of any of the City's livery companies. Its rich monumentality reflects the wealth of the company, which can trace its history back to the 12th century.

◄**1** St Lawrence Jewry: the magnificent sword-rest in front of the Lord Mayor's Pew. Sword-rests are designed to support the ceremonial sword of the Lord Mayor when he attends a church service. They came into use after 1660 and can be seen in several City churches. Initially they were made of wood, but almost all that survive are of iron. Many are decorated with the Lord Mayor's coat of arms (if he was entitled to bear one) and also that of his livery company. (See also **15**.)

Preface

The City of London is a square mile, or to be precise 675 acres, at the centre of England's capital. Its boundaries run from the Temple in the west to the Tower in the east and from the Thames northwards to the Barbican. Like Kensington, Westminster or Chelsea, it is an area with a very individual character. Yet there is something special about the City of London (or 'the City' as it is usually known), a combination of history and function that marks it out from London's other communities. For nearly ten centuries the City *was* London and it is rich in reminders of this long story. Today it is best known as England's financial centre, the home of the country's banking, insurance and mercantile interests. This busy world has imparted a unique flavour to the City, as well as giving it a leading international role.

The first part of this book explains how history has shaped the physical appearance of the City. So crowded during working days, in the evening and at weekends it is largely deserted, giving the visitor an opportunity for relaxed exploration of the fascinating architectural heritage illustrated here. The varied institutions of the modern City, their workings, ceremonies and traditions, are explained and discussed in the second section, completing a survey of the evolution of the City through two thousand years and showing its undiminished importance today.

◄2 *The Guildhall: the home of City government. The original 15th-century building has been much adapted; its present façade was designed by George Dance the Younger (1788–9). It is topped by the City coat of arms and motto 'Domine, dirige nos' ('Lord, guide us'). A modern extension (to the left of this picture) houses the Guildhall Library, which contains a superb collection relating to the history of London.*

History

The origins of London are obscure. According to legends that were largely invented by medieval historians, the city was founded by refugees from Troy. Their settlement was later named 'London' or 'Lud's Town' after the mythical King Lud, who reputedly built the walls and gates of the city (including Ludgate – still a street name of modern London) about 100 years before the Romans conquered Britain in AD 43. However, there is no evidence for a settlement of any significance on the site of the City of London before the Roman one. The new town was at once important, for it was on the lowest bridging point of the River Thames and on the highest point of the tidal river that could be reached by ship. From the beginning it was a major communications centre, for the Romans built the first bridge over the river (near the site of the present London Bridge), on which many of the country's newly constructed roads converged; and ships from the Continent usually came to the port of London because the Thames was the British estuary closest to Europe. The Romans called their new settlement 'Londinium', a word of partly Celtic origin which may derive from *lond*, meaning fierce or wild, or from a person called Londinos, or perhaps from a now lost tribal name.

The Roman settlement, constructed around the bridgehead, was described early in the 2nd century by the Roman historian Tacitus as 'a celebrated centre of commerce', but in AD 60 it was destroyed by the East Anglian tribe of the Iceni, led by their queen, Boudicca, in revenge for their treatment at the hands of the Roman Procurator. On the death of their king he had seized their property and his soldiers had flogged Boudicca and raped her daughters. The triumph of the Iceni was short-lived; they were soon routed by the far superior army of the Romans. But they had obliterated the first London, and evidence of the destruction, in the form of a layer of ashes and burnt clay, has been found during excavations in the area of Lombard and Gracechurch Streets.

The ease of the Iceni attack had made the need for adequate defences clear. Early in the 2nd century a fort covering an area of about 11 acres was built in the Cripplegate area. A more thorough protection came in *c.* 200, when a wall was built around the city in the form of an arc from the future site of the Tower in the east to the Blackfriars area in the west: this was to provide the boundaries of the city for the next thousand years and have a profound influence on its future development. Made of Kentish ragstone specially transported up the Thames, the wall was pierced by gates where major roads entered the city; parts of it can still be seen today, for example at Cooper's Row (**3**) and on Tower Hill (although the Roman masonry usually only survives to the modern ground level, anything above being medieval rebuilding). In 1976 a long-standing scholarly dispute was resolved when it was discovered that the Roman wall also ran along the river front.

◄ **3** *Fragment of the City wall at Cooper's Row, off Trinity Square. This is one of the most substantial surviving portions of the City wall, about 100 feet (30 metres) long and 35 feet (11 metres) high. Until 1961 it was incorporated into a now demolished 19th-century warehouse. The Roman wall, built in the 2nd century AD, survives to a height of about 13 feet (4 metres), rising just above the modern ground level. Above this is medieval rebuilding, which has been preserved to nearly its original height. Part of the parapet walk survives at the southern end, shown here.*

During the 4th century, as the fortunes of the Roman Empire began to fail, the prosperity of Londinium declined. In 410 the Emperor Honorius, frightened by the growing threat to his empire from the barbarians, ordered the withdrawal of Roman troops from Britain to defend Rome. The British were left to protect themselves against increasingly frequent raids by marauding parties of Saxons. In 457, so the Anglo-Saxon Chronicle relates, the men of Londinium received survivors of a battle fought in Kent against the Saxons under Hengist. For the next 150 years there is no mention of London in recorded history.

It is not clear what happened to London after the Romans left, but there is little evidence of actual destruction; it seems rather that since the Saxons did not at first centre their lives around towns, London was simply abandoned and lost all its importance as a centre of administration and trade. None the less, it was considered important enough to be chosen as the centre of Christianity in Britain by Pope Gregory, following Augustine's successful mission to convert the English. In 604 the first bishop of London, Mellitus, was appointed and the building of a church dedicated to St Paul began. However, London's conversion to Christianity initially proved short-lived; her citizens reverted to paganism, leaving Canterbury as the centre of Christianity in Britain, which it has remained ever since. Christianity returned to London in the 7th century; from 675 to 693 its bishop was Erkenwald, later canonized, whose tomb in St Paul's Cathedral was to be a popular place of pilgrimage throughout the Middle Ages. There were probably numerous other churches at this time; both All Hallows, Barking, and St Bride's, Fleet Street, have Saxon foundations.

But London was still not secure from attack. It was plagued by raiding parties of Danes from the end of the 8th century, and in 851 they seized the town with a great show of force. London remained under their control until King Alfred recaptured it in 886. Alfred unified the seven Saxon kingdoms, and he and his successors began a period of reconstruction and redevelopment, improving defences and expanding trade. But at the end of the 9th century Danish attacks began again and the rest of England finally submitted to them in 1015; London, however, held out, and in 1016 its citizens made a separate peace with the Danish leader, Cnut, accepting him as their king. When all England paid tribute to the new masters in 1018, London's contribution was £10,000, one-eighth of the total – an indication of its wealth and importance. In 1042, when Cnut's son died, Edward the Confessor became king. His decision to build an abbey and palace at Westminster initiated the dual development of the Cities of Westminster and London, the one becoming the political capital, the other the commercial centre. (In the following pages, London as a whole ('the city') is distinguished from the City of London ('the City').)

After his victory at Hastings in 1066, William the Conqueror advanced on London, for by now it was so important that any invader had to occupy and control it before he could be sure of possessing the country. Evidently William had some respect for its citizens' rights and privileges, for these are set out in a charter, still preserved in the Guildhall, that he granted them in return for acknowledging him as a king; but soon after his coronation he withdrew to Barking Abbey, according to a chronicle of his reign, 'while certain strongholds were made in the town against the fickleness of the vast and fierce population'. These strongholds included the White Tower (**62**), which now forms the nucleus of the Tower of London, and, in the west of the City, the now vanished Baynard's Castle and Tower of Montfichet. The citizens of London were not be

►**4** *St Bartholomew-the-Great, Smithfield: the chancel, looking west. The solemnly majestic interior of this 12th-century church is one of the most impressive examples of Norman architecture in London.*

allowed to forget their new king's power and authority – which they resented. Throughout the medieval period the Londoners, proud of their independence, strove to protect and increase their privileges, while the king, although anxious to secure the political and financial support of the citizens, tried to assert his authority. By the early 13th century the City had secured some important gains – such as the right to collect its own taxes and elect its own Mayor and Sheriffs – that were sometimes temporarily withdrawn but never permanently lost.

London was continually growing and by the early 13th century had reached the present City boundaries (see above, p. 5). Many of the streets of the modern City preserve memories of the medieval past, for they are named after the nationality or trade of those who lived and worked there. Thus Old Jewry is named after the Jewish ghetto which existed in the area until the Jews were expelled from England in 1290; Lombard Street takes it name from the Italian merchants who lived there, Fish Street Hill from its fishmongers and Milk and Bread Streets and Poultry from the products sold there. The City was full of markets, the main ones being at East Cheap and West Cheap (Cheapside); Cheapside was especially famous for the goldsmiths and jewellers who lived nearby. (The word 'cheap' in 'Cheapside' comes from the Anglo-Saxion *ceapian*, 'to buy'.)

Guilds and companies dominated the trades and crafts of medieval London. They had their origin in religious and social fraternities of Saxon times, which were often associated with a particular trade or craft. Gradually the companies gained for themselves various rights and privileges, often embodied in a charter of incorporation from the monarch, which secured their ascendancy over the City's trade. (For a detailed account of the guilds, and of their continued survival in the form of the livery companies, see below, pp. 54–60.) The guilds and companies were closely involved with City government, and by the 14th century the Mayor was nearly always elected from their ranks.

Religion played a central part in the life of medieval man, and London was full of churches: perhaps not as many as the 126 Fitzstephen claimed to exist, but certainly 97 – the number of parishes within the walls. Most of them must have been small towered buildings, rather like the 15th-century church of St Ethelburga, Bishopsgate, and probably not architecturally very significant. One splendid ancient church that has survived is St Bartholomew-the-Great, West Smithfield (**4**). It was founded in 1123 by Rahere, a courtier of Henry I, as a priory for an order of Augustinian canons, and it was one of the largest churches in the country. Much of the original building was allowed to decay after the Reformation and some of it was demolished, but today the parish church, despite later additions, basically consists of the chancel and crossing of the original priory church. It is an impressive example of Norman work, with great, plain rounded columns and arches. The Lady Chapel (of about 1330) has been put to a variety of uses, including, during the 18th century, a printer's workshop where the young Benjamin Franklin was employed. The Norman transepts were rebuilt in the 19th century. Few medieval fittings remain, but they include the only pre-Reformation font in the City, where the painter William Hogarth was baptized in 1697. On the south side of the chancel is an early 16th-century oriel window let into the choir from the rooms of Prior Bolton, so that he could watch Mass without actually having to attend. One of the panels bears his rebus (visual pun), a bolt piercing a barrel (tun). There are several interesting monuments; Rahere's own was not erected until *c.* 1500,

►**5** *St Helen's, Bishopsgate: the attractive west front of this 13th-century church has low-pitched gables and a 17th-century bell turret. The church is in a quiet position behind office blocks, only a few paces from the roar of traffic in Bishopsgate.*

although he died in 1143. There is an elaborate memorial to Sir Walter Mildmay and his wife; he was Chancellor to Elizabeth I and founder of Emmanuel College, Cambridge.

Nearby is St Bartholomew's Hospital, founded by Rahere at the same time as the priory and originally run by the canons. After the Reformation it was refounded by Henry VIII. Today it is one of the country's most famous teaching hospitals, popularly known as 'Barts'; it is also the oldest hospital in London still occupying its original site.

Most of the City's medieval churches were destroyed in the Great Fire of 1666. Among the few survivors is St Helen's, Bishopsgate (**5**). At one time this was two churches, hence its present curious arrangement; in the 13th century the church of a Benedictine convent was added to the north of the existing parish church, separated from it by a more solid screen than the slim arcade which now divides the buildings. The proximity of the outside world seems to have distracted the nuns from their vocations, for in 1385 they were warned to 'abstain from kissing secular persons, a custom to which they have become too prone'. In the nuns' part of the church is a squint through which they could watch services in the parish church. Famous for its brasses, St Helen's also contains one of the finest collections of memorials and tombs in the City. Among them are the tombs of Sir John Crosby and his wife, owners of Crosby Hall, formerly nearby; the tomb of Sir Julius Caesar, a judge, carved by Nicholas Stone in 1636 (there is no effigy, simply a legal document with its seal carved on a tomb chest); and the severely simple monument of Sir Thomas Gresham, founder of the Royal Exchange (see below, p. 18), a striking contrast with the

The Olde Wine Shades
established here since 1663
•
Come in for wines,
Spirits or liqueurs
GLASS,
BOTTLE,
or **CASK.**

The only City Tavern to survive
The Great Fire of 1666.
A wine shop in the old style
frequented by Charles Dickens

EL VINO CO. LTD.

◄ 8 *St Olave's, Hart Street: the memorial to the Bayninge brothers – Andrew (died 1610), an Alderman of the City, and Paul (died 1616), an Alderman and Sheriff – at the eastern end of this 15th-century church. The diarist Samuel Pepys and his wife, Elizabeth, are buried here. The 17th-century churchyard gate from Seething Lane has skulls carved on it, which caused Dickens, in his story 'The Uncommercial Traveller', to refer to St Olave's as 'St Ghastly Grim'.*

► 9 *The doorway of St Katharine Cree, Leadenhall Street. This is one of the few early 17th-century churches in England (its tower, built in 1504, is from an earlier building). It was consecrated in 1631 by Archbishop Laud with much elaborate ceremonial and ritual – which provided one of the charges at his trial in 1644. The interior combines Corinthian columns carrying arches with a Gothic rib-vault, and the painted bosses of the vault bear the arms of City livery companies. The arms of the Gayer family can be seen on the 17th-century font; Sir John Gayer left an endowment for the 'Lion Sermon', still preached here annually, to commemorate his escape from a lion while travelling in Arabia.*

opulent memorial to Sir William Pickering (1574). Many of the church's fittings are 17th century, including the font and a very rare wooden sword rest of 1665 (almost all the sword rests in the City are of iron and much later).

The glory of medieval London was old St Paul's, one of the largest cathedrals in the country, with a nave 585 feet (178 metres) long, and a tall wooden spire of 489 feet (149 metres) dominating the skyline. It was a mixture of styles, as building began in 1087 (the first church had been destroyed by fire) and was not finished until 1240. A Gothic choir and further additions followed in the 13th and 14th centuries, and there were many ecclesiastical buildings in the surrounding precinct.

Besides being the religious centre of the City, St Paul's was the traditional venue of the folkmoot, a meeting of all the citizens, at which announcements relating to City affairs were made and important business discussed. The folkmoot declined during the Middle Ages because City government became more complex as trade and population increased. By the 12th century (and possibly earlier) the City was divided, as it is today, into administrative units known as wards. Their origin is unclear; in some cases they may have evolved from manors in private hands. The chief citizen in each ward was known as an Alderman, and gradually City government passed into the control of the few as the Aldermen took charge of administration and began to hold regular meet-

ings, known as the Court of Hustings (*husting* is the Anglo-Saxon word for a place of assembly).

Aldermanbury, where the Guildhall stands, is an area long associated with City government. A Guildhall is first referred to in writing in 1120, but we do not know where it was or what it was like. The present Guildhall (**2**) was built 1411–40, and although it has suffered much damage and been restored many times, one can still admire the original work. The hall, 150 feet (46 metres) long, was one of the most splendid in medieval London. It was used for civic business and for important trials, including, in 1553, the trial of Lady Jane Grey, the nine-day queen. The porch and much of the masonry are original. After bombing in World War II the Guildhall was restored by Sir Giles Gilbert Scott, who gave it a stone arched roof resembling the one the medieval building is believed to have possessed. At the west end of the hall stand the famous figures of Gog and Magog, who, according to legend, fought battles for the Trojans against the British natives. They were initially known as Gogmagog and Corienus, the former representing the inhabitants of Britain and the latter the invaders, but subsequently (probably after the 16th century) the names were changed. The statues replace 18th-century ones destroyed in 1940, which purported to be copies of effigies used during medieval pageants. Today the Guildhall is decorated with the banners of the principal livery companies and monuments to national figures. Below the Guildhall is the most extensive medieval crypt in London, dating from the 15th century, with impressive vaulting in blue Purbeck marble.

The main dangers facing medieval Londoners were fire, which often broke out in the narrow crowded alleys that filled the City, the buildings being mainly of timber, wattle and thatch; endemic violence between rival groups of apprentices that frequently resulted in sudden death (and also erupted between citizens and some of the many groups of foreigners living in the City); and disease, especially Bubonic plague, which had its most virulent outbreak in the Black Death of 1348–9 (there are no precise figures for London itself, but in the country as a whole one person in three died).

In 1381 occurred one of the most dramatic events in the history of the City, the so-called Peasants' Revolt. Groups of rebels led by Wat Tyler, protesting against increases in taxation, marched on the City to demand justice from the youthful Richard II. They were let into the City by Aldermen and apprentices who sympathized with their cause, and at once set to burning and looting. Then they dragged the much-hated Archbishop of Canterbury, Simon Sudbury, from the Tower and beheaded him on Tower Hill. Finally they met the king at Smithfield, where the Mayor, William Walworth, killed Wat Tyler with a dagger still preserved in Fishmongers' Hall. Unnerved, the rebels went away quietly after Richard promised to remedy their grievances. He never did.

The 16th century saw great changes in the City. Many are recorded in John Stow's famous *Survey of London* (1598), the first detailed topographical description of the city. The population increased dramatically, but overcrowding in the City was eased slightly by the release of ecclesiastical land following the Dissolution of the monasteries in the 1530s. The religious houses were sold to private buyers and put to a variety of uses: the Minories was converted from a convent into a gunpowder store; Greyfriars became a school (Christ's Hospital). Others, such as the Charterhouse (**6**), which lies just outside the City boundaries, were demolished and their materials re-used for private residences. The

►**10** *The Monument, built 1671–7 to the designs of Wren and Hooke, commemorates the Great Fire (1666). This tall Doric column of white Portland stone now stands amid a new phase of redevelopment in the City, much of it occasioned by the bombs of World War II. It is 202 feet (62 metres) high and situated 202 feet away from the spot in Pudding Lane where the Great Fire began. The view from the top is well worth the climb (311 steps). The Monument is surmounted by a square balcony with a brass urn and gilded flaming ball resting on a dome; Wren wished to have a statue of Charles II, but the king refused because, it was said, he feared people might assume he had started the Fire. An inscription celebrates the rebuilding of the City: 'Three short years complete what was the work of an age'. This is something of an exaggeration: reconstruction actually took a quarter of a century.*

mansion which Sir Edward North made of the Charterhouse still survives. The Great Hall is early Elizabethan, with a hammerbeam roof and minstrels' gallery. The Great Chamber dates from about 1571. The chapel, built on the site of the chapter house, contains an elaborate monument to Thomas Sutton, who bought the Charterhouse in 1611; he left an endowment for the foundation of a charity school (the beginning of the famous boys' school which moved from here to its present site in Godalming, Surrey, in 1872). He also endowed an almshouse for 80 gentlemen pensioners, which still exists here, although now the charity can only support 40.

For many of its inhabitants 16th-century London was a prosperous place. The arrival in the City of foreign artisans, many of them fleeing religious persecution on the Continent, stimulated the production of finer and more elaborate goods. New trading companies were set up, incorporated by royal charter. The Muscovey Company (1553) and the East India Company (1600) were both designed to develop the markets made accessible by new sea routes and the general expansion of maritime traffic. Commercial considerations also lay behind the largest building project the City embarked on during these years: the Royal Exchange. This was erected at the expense of Sir Thomas Gresham, a wealthy mercer, who believed it was essential for the City to have a building like the Antwerp Bourse, where merchants could meet and discuss and conduct their business. The Corporation presented Gresham with a site between Cornhill and Threadneedle Streets, and the building was opened by Queen Elizabeth in 1571. With the decline of Amsterdam in the 17th century, the

►*12 St Paul's Cathedral: the chancel. At the east end is the High Altar and an oak baldacchino made after World War II to designs by Wren. The mosaics in the spandrels of the dome and vaults were added in the 19th century: much has been done in recent years to restore the original appearance of the building.*

▼*11 St Paul's Cathedral from the south-east. The dome of Wren's masterpiece is a remarkable feat as much of engineering as of architecture. The drum carries an immense weight: the lantern and cross weigh 700 tons, while the dome itself weighs approximately 64,000 tons.*

14 *St Paul's dome, the innermost of three, is built of brick. Wren wished its interior to be decorated with mosaics, but the cost was found to be prohibitive, so Sir James Thornhill painted these frescoes (1716–19) depicting scenes from the life of St Paul.*

13 *St Paul's choir stalls show Grinling Gibbons's wood-carving skills at their finest. Cherubs' heads break forward from the scrolls of the frieze at the top; below them are rich festoons of flowers and fruit. Canopies mark the bishop's throne and Lord Mayor's seat.*

Royal Exchange became one of Northern Europe's main commercial centres. Gresham's building was destroyed in the Great Fire (1666); the present Royal Exchange was built 1841–4 (**25**).

The appearance of London was altered dramatically in 1561 when St Paul's steeple was struck by lightning and burnt down. It was never rebuilt, despite contributions for its repair by the queen and many wealthy citizens. The whole cathedral had deteriorated during the later Middle Ages, partly because it had come to be used as a general meeting-place, where lawyers and (before the building of the Royal Exchange) merchants congregated, and servants could be hired. In the mid-16th century ordinances were issued to prevent horses being led through the cathedral, but it was still used as a short cut by those on foot.

St Paul's churchyard and many of the surrounding streets formed one of the main centres of London's bookselling and publishing trade – and remained so until World War II. Most of Shakespeare's works published during his lifetime were issued from here. Some of his plays were performed at Blackfriars Theatre, which stood nearby, in what is now Playhouse Yard. It was one of the two homes of the King's Men, the company of actors to which Shakespeare belonged; it was an indoor theatre, unlike the Globe, their theatre on the other side of the river. Both theatres were sited in areas where the Lord Mayor had no jurisdiction, for the City Corporation, influenced by the Puritans, disapproved of play-acting and the rowdy crowds it often attracted. After the Blackfriars was demolished in 1655 there was no theatre within the City boundaries until the opening of the Mermaid Theatre in 1959.

Few City buildings survive from the 16th and early 17th centuries. Of those that have gone, one of the most important was the Palace of Bridewell, built near Blackfriars by Henry VIII. Edward VI gave it to the City as a hospital and it was also used as a house of correction, and finally as a warehouse, before its demolition. Many streets must have contained buildings like those of Staple Inn, High Holborn, with its impressive (much restored) half-timbered façade. Another piece of fine timber work is the Inner Temple Gateway, Fleet Street (1610–11); on the first floor is a large room with one of the best Jacobean plaster ceilings in London. The Prince of Wales's feathers and the initials PH in the centre of the ceiling have given rise to the theory that the room was used by Prince Henry, eldest son of James I. Prince Henry's Room, as it is now known, houses an exhibition of material relating to the life of Samuel Pepys.

After the end of the 16th century many wealthy noblemen began to desert their City homes, moving westwards to new and more fashionable developments. This left the City to the merchants and tradesmen and widened the gap between the court and the City at a time when relations between the two were already strained. Both James I and Charles I were continually in financial difficulty and some of their methods of raising money were disapproved of by the City fathers, who also felt that the Crown did not do enough to encourage trade. During the struggles of the Civil War the majority of the City's leaders supported the Parliamentary cause and the City remained a Roundhead stronghold throughout the conflict. The large sums of money it provided contributed greatly towards the eventual Parliamentary victory, and in the eyes of one Royalist, 'If posterity shall ask who would have pulled the Crown from the King's head . . . say, "twas the proud, unthankful, schismatical, rebellious, bloody, City of London".'

The events that dominate the City's history in the second half of the 17th century are the Great Plague of 1665 and the Great Fire of the following year. There are vivid accounts of both in the diaries of Samuel Pepys and John Evelyn. Bubonic plague, spread by fleas carried by the black rat, had been recurrent in England since the early Middle Ages; the Great Plague was the last major outbreak and one of the most virulent. The first case was reported in May 1665 in the parish of St Giles-in-the-Fields, just outside the City walls, and the disease spread at an alarming rate during the hot summer. No one knew how to curb it or how to treat it. Life in the City was brought to a halt. Those who were able, left for the countryside; for months the deserted streets echoed to the sound of carts carrying the dead away. Many were buried in a huge open grave near Aldgate. In one parish alone, St Bride's, 2000 people died, and in London as a whole about one third of the population perished.

Inevitably, fire was a fairly common occurrence in a city built mainly of wood, so at first little attention was paid to the outbreak on the night of 1 September 1666 at the home of a baker in Pudding Lane. But the weather had been hot and dry and there was a strong easterly wind. The fire spread rapidly, and raged out of control once it reached the warehouses lining the river, which were full of combustible materials. No concerted effort was made to stop it, partly because the Lord Mayor feared the consequences of pulling down houses in its path. It blazed on for three days, consuming everything that lay in its way – houses, livery halls, churches, the Guildhall, even St Paul's Cathedral. Charles II and his brother the Duke of York worked tirelessly to supervise the firefighters, and eventually, with the help of sailors from the docks, blew up rows of houses to create gaps that the fire could not cross. This, together with

►15 *St Lawrence Jewry, designed by Christopher Wren, replaces a church lost in the Great Fire. It is now the official church of the City Corporation (replacing the Guildhall's chapel, demolished in 1820). Several official services are held here during the year, including the Court of Common Council service in January and the service held before the election of the Lord Mayor on Michaelmas Day (29 September).*

the dying of the wind, at last caused the fire to abate on the night of Wednesday 5 September. It had devastated 436 acres, 300 of them within the City walls. 'I went to the ruins, for it was no longer a city', wrote Evelyn in his diary.

Everything had been brought to a standstill, but prompt action was taken to provide temporary accommodation for the thousands of refugees at Moorfields. Within days a proclamation was issued in the king's name stating various conditions for rebuilding. These included the provisos that all new buildings be of brick or stone, and that all new thoroughfares be wide enough for the easy passage of vehicles. Christopher Wren – who was at this date better known as an astronomer than as an architect, though he had already designed the Sheldonian Theatre in Oxford and Pembroke College Chapel at Cambridge – produced a plan for a new model City, regularly laid out with wide streets and elegant buildings. But neither this nor other ambitious designs, including one for rebuilding the City in the form of an exact parallelogram, ever reached fruition. The cost, the immediate needs of those made homeless and the pressure to start trade again made any major changes impossible; and so the City, although much improved by the new regulations, on the whole retained its medieval ground plan.

Both the Crown and the City Corporation appointed commissioners to supervise rebuilding, including Wren, the architect Sir Roger Pratt, the builder Edward Jerman and the scientist Robert Hooke. Many of the worst of the old narrow alleys disappeared, two new thoroughfares were made (King and Queen Streets) and most of the buildings were much sounder than those they replaced. For the first time, stone and brick were the predominant building materials. The reconstruction of the City took many years to complete and corresponded with a change in its population: many citizens chose not to return, deterred by high rents charged for the new buildings, or because they preferred the pleasant suburbs to the grimy, crowded town, or because they wished to avoid the restrictions imposed upon craftsmen in the City by the livery companies.

The fire is commemorated by Wren and Robert Hooke's Monument (**10**), a huge Roman Doric column which rises 202 feet (62 metres) above Fish Street – the distance from the base of the Monument to the site of the baker's house where the fire started. The Monument is decorated with an allegorical relief showing Charles II in Roman dress encouraging his people to rebuild the City; an inscription attributing the fire to papal malice was not removed until 1831.

The magnificent climax of Wren's work in the City is London's cathedral, St Paul's. Old St Paul's had continued to deteriorate after the damage by lightning, and in the 1630s the celebrated architect Inigo Jones was commissioned to restore it. His main contribution was to add a large classical portico to the west end, impressive in itself, but rather out of keeping with the Gothic cathedral. All restoration work ceased during the Civil War and during the Interregnum much of St Paul's was used as a barracks. Plans for future repairs were underway when the Great Fire broke out; ironically, the scaffolding in which the cathedral was shrouded, so that a survey of its fabric could be made, helped the fire to spread. St Paul's was not completely destroyed, and at first there was some hope that it could be repaired, but this proved to be impracticable.

Once the decision had been taken to rebuild St Paul's Wren submitted several designs that were rejected. One of the more interesting survives in the form of the wooden 'Great Model', to be seen in the cathedral's crypt; it is in the form of a Greek cross and was disliked by the clergy, who wanted a traditional long nave. Finally, in 1675, consent was given by royal warrant to what became known as the Warrant Design. In several ways this was inferior to the others – for instance, Wren proposed an odd, tall spire on top of the dome. Luckily, however, it was agreed that should Wren wish to make alterations 'ornamental rather than essential' he could do so, and he interpreted this allowance boldly, making radical modifications to the design in execution.

The exterior of the cathedral (**11**) conveys solidity and grandeur; the high, two-storied walls, decorated with Corinthian pillars and pilasters below and Composite ones above, give the impression that this is an aisleless building. But in fact the upper part of the wall is false: it was designed by Wren to disguise the difference in height between nave and aisles and to conceal the flying buttresses which help support the weight of the vaults. The clerestory windows of the nave and choir are actually several feet behind this wall and are invisible from the ground. The external walls are rich in detail and ornamentation; for example, the small panels below the round-arched windows of the nave, transepts and choir have delicate carving, and beneath the lower entablature that runs round the building there are festoons of fruit and floral garlands carved in stone.

Both the north and south transepts have beautiful semi-circular porticos; on the pediment of that on the south is Cibber's relief sculpture of a phoenix rising, with the inscription 'Resurgam'. It is said that when Wren was working out the position of the new building a workman handed him a fragment of one of the old cathedral's headstones, bearing the single word *Resurgam* (I shall rise again). The west front of the cathedral has an imposing portico with two tiers of coupled columns; the relief on the pediment above depicts the conversion of St Paul. This front has formed the backdrop to many scenes of national celebration, including Queen Victoria's Diamond Jubilee in 1897 and the wedding of the Prince of Wales and Lady Diana Spencer in 1981.

The west portico is flanked by two graceful towers of complex design, which admirably complement the simplicity of the majestic dome, still the most beautiful feature of London's skyline. Wren was influenced by designs for the dome of St Peter's, Rome, but St Paul's dome has a quality of serene, classical repose which is entirely his own. It is in fact not one dome but two, for the inner dome is not large enough to appear sufficiently impressive from the outside, so Wren devised an ample outer dome, consisting only of a skin of lead on a timber framework. As neither dome could support the beautiful Baroque stone lantern that tops Wren's creation, a brick cone was inserted between the two domes, hidden from both inside and out, to take the strain of the lantern's weight.

As one enters the cathedral, the eye is drawn along the full length of the building, through the choir to the High Altar. The 20th-century baldacchino, based on designs by Wren, replaces a rather hideous Victorian reredos destroyed in World War II. On a sunny day, light pours into the building through the large semi-circular clerestory windows, making the honey-coloured limestone of the interior glow. The focus of the building is the great central space below the dome. From here the openings to the nave, transepts and choir can be seen to be higher than those to their aisles; to obtain eight arches of even height on which to rest his dome, Wren added a high balconied opening above the low arches. The resulting effect is complicated and perhaps not entirely successful. The dome is decorated with frescoes (Wren wanted mosaics) by Sir James Thornhill of scenes from the life of St Paul (**14**). About 100 feet (30 metres) from

► **17** *St Margaret Lothbury. Wren's church of 1686–90 replaces an early medieval building. The richly furnished interior is dominated by the superb chancel screen, made for the now demolished All Hallows the Great, to which it was presented by a German merchant, Theodore Jacobsen. The brass chandeliers are typical of 17th-century church interiors.*

◄ **18** *St Mary-le-Bow,
Cheapside. The
magnificent tower and
steeple are set forward
from the church because
Wren wished to use a
Roman gravel roadway as
foundation. The steeple,
one of Wren's best known,
is especially sumptuous —
it cost almost as much as
the rest of the church. It is
topped by a huge copper
weather vane in the form
of a griffin, the City's
symbol. The tower, which
contains the famous Bow
bells, survived fire and the
collapse of the bells during
World War II. The
tower's balcony, facing
the street, is a reminder of
the viewing gallery which
stood outside the medieval
church, from which
royalty and the nobility
could watch ceremonial
processions.*

the ground around the edge of the dome is the Whispering Gallery, so called because freak acoustics enable even such a faint sound as a whisper to travel around the wall and be heard on the other side of the gallery.

The fittings of the cathedral are of the highest quality, and luckily survived bomb damage to the cathedral in World War II more or less intact. Much of the wood carving is by the renowned Grinling Gibbons, and here his work can be seen at its most superb in the exquisite carving of the choir stalls, organ case and screens (**12, 13**). The ironwork is also magnificent; it is mostly by a Huguenot refugee, Jean Tijou, and includes the screens at the entrances to the chancel aisles. The organ was built by Bernhard Schmidt ('Father' Smith) in 1694; it was played by Handel.

Until the 1790s most of the cathedral's few monuments were in the crypt. It was then decided to place four statues of national luminaries in front of the crossing piers, under the dome. They are Sir Joshua Reynolds, Samuel Johnson (plainly embarrassed by his unbecoming toga), the prison reformer John Howard, and the orientalist Sir William Jones. They were the outriders of an army of Neoclassical military and naval heroes, the honoured men of the campaigns against Napoleon. The best is Flaxman's monument to Nelson (1808–18) in the south transept: Britannia presents two young cadets from Dartmouth Naval College to the vigorously characterized Nelson, watched by a lion. The masterly Wellington Monument, dominating the north aisle of the nave, is by Alfred Stevens, although it was not finished (with the completion of the duke's equestrian statue) until 1912, 37 years after Stevens's death. Poor Stevens constantly had to battle against officials who conspired to cut his budget; as a revenge, the face of Discord in the group 'Truth plucking out the tongue of Falsehood' was modelled on the government's mean finance minister. The only monument from the old cathedral to survive the fire intact is that of the poet John Donne, who was dean of St Paul's 1621–31, by Nicholas Stone. It stands in a niche in the south choir aisle and shows Donne dressed in his shroud (in which he posed for the sculptor during his lifetime).

The foundation stone of the cathedral was laid in 1675; in 1711 the building was declared complete by Parliament, and Wren, by then aged 79, had lived to see his masterpiece finished. But during the final years of construction his relations with the commission which had appointed him and which oversaw the work were not happy. He was blamed, perhaps unfairly considering the number of projects he was involved in, for the slow progress of the building, and his meagre salary (£200 a year) was suspended as an incentive to faster work. He was annoyed by Thornhill's painting of the dome and by the addition, against his wishes, of a balustrade around the building ('Ladies think nothing well without an edging', he declared bitterly). Finally, in 1718, he was cursorily dismissed from his post as Surveyor General. But the cathedral remains his personal triumph and greatest achievement. As the famous epitaph on his movingly simple memorial in the crypt says, 'Lector, si monumentum requiris, circumspice' (Reader, if you seek his monument, look around you).

Most of the new City that rose from the ashes of the Fire was destroyed in subsequent rebuilding or by the bombs of World War II. Today it is epitomized in the surviving churches designed by Wren; after St Paul's they are the City's chief architectural glory. Of the 86 churches gutted in the Fire it was decided to rebuild 51, and Wren was appointed Surveyor General to the Church Commissioners with overall responsibility for design. Obviously he could not supervise every detail of the execution, so he built up a team of skilled assistants and craftsmen to help him. The reconstruction was financed by a tax on all coal coming into the City, but fittings for the individual churches were paid for by their vestries or by private benefactors.

In many instances Wren's task was complicated by having to build the churches more or less on their old sites, which were often cramped and irregularly shaped. But within this limitation he created a remarkable diversity of designs, influenced by the fashion for centrally planned churches and by his own belief that in the reformed religion those present at a service should both see and hear everything. His designs are of two main types: a traditional oblong with nave and aisles, such as St Bride's, Fleet Street, and a small square, such as St Mary Abchurch, Abchurch Lane. As the churches were frequently built against on at least three sides, there was little scope for exterior decoration, so from the outside it is the towers and spires of lead and stone that give the churches their individuality and chief ornament. The beautifully various skyline they once created is now obscured by later buildings but was captured in the paintings of several artists, notably Canaletto (1697–1768). Interior fittings for the churches, often superb, were the work of numerous craftsmen, the most famous being Grinling Gibbons (although his work for the City churches was fairly limited). Unfortunately many of these fittings were removed in the 19th century, when Wren and classical ecclesiastical architecture were deeply unfashionable. Still more were lost in the Blitz, so that now it is seldom possible to gain an exact impression of all Wren's intentions for the interiors, though much outstanding work remains.

Today 23 of Wren's churches survive. Several were demolished during the 19th century, as the number of City parishioners dwindled. Money was needed for building new churches in London's growing suburbs, and to the Church it seemed logical to sell the by now very valuable sites of the under-used buildings, regardless of architectural value. A further attempt to reduce their numbers, in the 1920s, was largely foiled, but the bombs of 1940–1 succeeded where the bishops had failed. In some cases restoration of war damage was possible; elsewhere often only a tower remains. As they now serve only very small numbers of parishioners, many of the churches have been designated Guild Churches. They are without parochial duties and are usually closed on Sundays, but open during the week for a variety of events: their frequent lunch-time services and concerts are well attended by City workers.

A selection of the churches will give an idea of their quality and diversity. The delightful St Benet's, Paul's Wharf, in Upper Thames Street, home of the Welsh Episcopalians since the late 19th century, now stands isolated after recent demolitions. Its attractive exterior is more elaborate than that of most other City churches and shows strong Dutch influence in the hipped roof, the warm brickwork with quoins of Portland limestone and the stone garlands decorating the round-headed windows. The interior, nearly square, is one of the least spoiled, and has changed little since its completion in 1685 – it has even kept its galleries, which is very rare, though the box pews have been cut down. It is rich in woodwork and its fittings include a doorcase with the arms of Charles II carved above, an elaborate communion table, and an octagonal font. As the parish includes the nearby College of Arms (see below, p. 74), many of the church's monuments are memorials to heralds.

St James Garlickhythe, Garlick Hill, is so called, according to Stow, because

► **19** *The Jamaica Wine House, St Michael's Alley, lies in one of the maze of alleyways between Cornhill and Lombard Street. It was built in 1688 as a coffee-house and was patronized by merchants concerned in trade with the West Indies, especially Jamaica. It was from such coffee-houses that many of the City's great financial institutions grew.*

garlic was formerly sold on the bank of the Thames here. The present church (1676–83) was originally isolated from other buildings, so the design is more symmetrical than some; it has one of Wren's most charming spires, in several stages with projecting Ionic columns at the angles of the lower stages. Inside, two rows of six Ionic columns form a nave and aisles. The aisles are very narrow, but they allowed Wren to build a high nave with clerestory windows, creating an interior so light and airy that the church is often called 'Wren's lantern'. St James's contains much woodwork, some original – the carved communion table, the churchwardens' pews and the organ case – and some from other Wren churches, including the pulpit (from St Michael Queenhithe) and doorcases now forming screens behind the choir stalls. It also retains some original ironwork, notably a swordrest and hat-stands. The mummified body of an unidentified man, found under the chancel and dubbed 'Jimmy Garlick', rests in a cupboard at the west end of the church. Although not one of Wren's best-known works, St James's illustrates more clearly than many of the other churches his original intentions.

St Stephen Walbrook is among Wren's most beautiful and subtle buildings. The exterior is fairly plain, but has an attractive spire surmounting the tower; the interior is exquisite. Although the building is an oblong, Wren has contrived a centralized cruciform arrangement by means of 16 Corinthian columns. Eight arches spring from the eight central columns, supporting a dome of plaster and wood that dominates the church. Light floods down from the lantern and windows to illumine one of the most complex and satisfying of Wren's ecclesiastical interiors. Although all the pews have been removed, much excellent woodwork remains, including a richly carved wine-glass pulpit – paid for, like many of the fittings, by the Grocers' Company. A painting by the only American president of the Royal Academy, Benjamin West's *The Burial of St Stephen* (1776), hangs in the church. In 1953, the now world-famous organization of the Samaritans was founded in the crypt of St Stephen's by the Reverend Chad Varrah, and this remains its headquarters.

One of Wren's largest and most expensive churches, St Lawrence Jewry (**1**, **15**), Gresham Street, was almost completely destroyed in December 1940. Virtually everything was lost, including some of the City's finest plasterwork, but the church has been skillfully rebuilt. The exterior is rather irregularly shaped; the west end, now opened up, was not intended by Wren to be visible. The splendid east end, which looks so superb from the Guildhall and King Street, is among Wren's richest compositions: Corinthian columns, flanked by pilasters, support a noble pediment.

St Margaret Lothbury (**17**, **26**) stands opposite the Bank of England. Again the exterior of the church is plain, but the tower is crowned by one of Wren's prettiest lead steeples. The interior, an irregular oblong, consists of nave, chancel and an aisle to the south that was made into a chapel in 1891 and is now separated from the main body of the church by a screen made from the altar rails of the demolished church of St Olave Jewry. St Margaret's has some of the most beautiful fittings in the City, including several pieces from demolished Wren churches. Amongst them is one of two surviving Wren screens (the other is in St Peter Cornhill), from All Hallows the Great. This is a superb piece of wood-carving, supported on delicate openwork balusters, with a huge majestic eagle hanging over the chancel entrance. Also notable is the reredos with Corinthian columns carrying two segmented pediments, the beautiful font (sometimes ascribed to Grinling Gibbons) and font cover, and the finely carved pulpit, from St Olave's, with a large tester, from All Hallows.

The most famous of all the City churches is probably St Mary-le-Bow (**18**); it is also one of the earliest – Wren's building rests on a Norman crypt, whose round arches or 'bows' gave the church its name. They also gave their name to the ecclesiastical Court of Arches, which continues to meet here. This is a court of the Archbishop of Canterbury, used for Church trials and appointments. The steeple is over 200 feet (61 metres) high, a particularly fine and elaborate design. It stands on a tower that dominates Cheapside and houses the famous Bow bells, which used to be rung every night as a curfew; it is said that only those born within hearing of them are true Cockneys. ('Cockney' is the Middle English for a 'cock's egg', a small malformed egg, and came to denote first a coddled child, then a simpleton, then a townsman ignorant of country matters, and eventually, in the 17th century, a Londoner, especially one from the City itself.) Both steeple and bells are reconstructions, for they came crashing down when the church was bombed in 1941; the bells were first rung again by Prince Philip in December 1961. The church's modern fittings include pleasing stained glass by John Hayward, who also designed the hanging rood.

While Wren was at work, a new and important institution began to appear in the City: the coffee-house. Places where men could drink the newly popular beverage and discuss business sprang up in great numbers, especially in the area of the Royal Exchange. Most of them have long disappeared, but one that still remains, though now a pub, is the Jamaica Wine House, St Michael's Alley, Cornhill (1688) (**19**). The oak-panelled interior has much of the appearance of an 18th-century coffee-house. Soon certain coffee-houses became associated with particular areas of business; men interested in trade with China or India tended to meet at the Jerusalem, while those involved in shipping and insurance would go to Edward Lloyd's – the start of what is now the world's leading insurance concern, Lloyd's of London (see below, pp. 73–4). Many other major City institutions emerged from such informal beginnings, including the Stock Exchange and the Baltic Exchange (see below, pp. 69–72).

The great trading companies set up in the 16th and 17th centuries grew in wealth and prestige during these years. The East India, Levant and Hudson Bay Companies exercised a virtual monopoly of trade in the areas allotted to them by their respective charters. London continued to flourish as a port, and became the hub of the country's overseas trade. At the end of the 17th century the City's first banks were founded; they were private institutions, such as Child's and Hoare's, but in 1694, after years of debate, a national bank, the Bank of England, was granted a charter by the government in return for a loan (see below, pp. 64–6). The City was gradually but steadily emerging as a national and international centre of finance and commerce.

Despite this new prosperity and many new and elegant buildings, early 18th-century London was also a city of poverty and squalor – the London that John Gay depicted in *The Beggar's Opera* and Hogarth luridly portrayed in such pictures as *Gin Lane*. Gin was a major pleasure and perhaps the chief affliction of the poor; it has been estimated that there were 826 licensed gin houses within the City by the end of the century – considerably fewer, even so, than there had been during the peak period 50 years earlier, before the tax on gin was raised.

There were still several prisons within the City, including the notorious Newgate, which was given an imposing new building by George Dance the

▶ **21** *College Hill: this splendid late 17th-century gateway, with its rich carving on the pediment, leads to a small courtyard containing a fine 18th-century brick house. College Hill is closely associated with Dick Whittington, who lived in a mansion on the site of nos. 19–20; he was buried in the nearby church of St Michael Paternoster Royal, destroyed in the Great Fire.*

◄22 *St Mary Woolnoth (1716–27), designed by Nicholas Hawksmoor. The interior is small but highly impressive. The excellent furnishings include this elaborate reredos; the placing of the Ten Commandments behind the altar is characteristic of post-Reformation churches. The ex-slave-trader John Newton, rector 1780–1807 and author, with Cowper, of the 'Olney Hymns', preached from the splendid pulpit, inspiring philanthropic reformers.*

OVERLEAF

23 *(left) Nos. 27–8 Queen Street, one of the best of the few remaining groups of 18th-century houses in the City, shaded by London Plane trees. This hybrid between the Oriental Plane and the American Plane was first planted in England in the late 17th century. Its success in even highly polluted city air is due to its habit of shedding part of its bark, with the sooty accretions, each year, and to its hard, glossy leaves, which are easily washed clean by rain, as well as to the ability of its roots to accommodate to inhospitable conditions.*

24 *(right) St Botolph Aldgate (1714–44), designed by George Dance the Elder. In 1889 the interior was redecorated in a free Gothic style by J. F. Bentley, the architect of Westminster Cathedral. Monuments include memorials to two victims of Henry VIII, Lord Darcey and Sir Nicholas Carew.*

Younger in 1770. Public executions, always popular spectacles, were held there until 1868. The prison was destroyed (though soon rebuilt) during the Gordon Riots of 1780, when vast anti-Catholic mobs stormed the capital, destroying the property of well-known Catholics and attacking public buildings, including the Bank of England, which was saved only by the quick action of troops stationed at the Royal Exchange. Other prisons included the debtors' prison, called the Fleet – reputedly the largest brothel in the country – and Ludgate. Bethlehem Hospital for lunatics, popularly known as 'Bedlam', stood on the southern side of Moorfields, with two large figures representing Melancholy and Raving Madness over the gates. Here many visitors to 18th-century London came to view the inmates for a small fee. Nearby in this rather disreputable area was Grub Street (renamed Milton Street in 1830), the home of many struggling writers. It was made famous by the definition in Dr Johnson's *Dictionary*: 'the name of a street in London much inhabited by writers of small histories, dictionaries and temporary poems, whence any mean product is called Grub Street'.

Although the City's population was declining, the City Corporation repeatedly refused to take any responsibility for the rapidly growing suburbs; however in the latter part of the century it did undertake various improvements to make the City cleaner and safer. Visitors had continually complained of the ill-lit, badly paved and smelly streets, described by a London newspaper in 1748 as 'a Hotch Potch of half moon and serpentine narrow streets, close dismal long lanes, stinking alleys, dark gloomy courts and suffocating yards'; there were also instances in the early 18th century of highwaymen robbing coaches even within the City boundaries. In the 1760s most of the remaining parts of the City wall that had stood for over 1500 years were pulled down, as were the City gates, which were now obsolete as a means of defence and hindered traffic. After the executions that followed the Jacobite Rebellion of 1745 heads of victims were no longer displayed on Temple Bar, although the last one was left decomposing there until 1772.

Until the 18th century the Lord Mayor had to hold office from his own house or from rented accommodation. This was remedied with the construction of an official residence, Mansion House, designed by George Dance the Elder (1739). It is an imposing building of Portland stone, Palladian in inspiration; the huge Corinthian pillars support a pediment decorated with a sculpture by Robert Taylor representing the Dignity and Opulence of the City, which is personified, leading in Plenty while treading Envy underfoot. Inside are the Lord Mayor's private apartments and the sumptuous state rooms, including the famous Egyptian Hall, richly decorated and impressively tall and long (90 feet – 27 metres). Examples of more modest domestic architecture of this date can still be seen in the City, though widely scattered and mostly converted into offices. One of the best examples is nos. 1–2 Laurence Pountney Hill, built in 1703 (**20**). From later in the century there is Crescent (1767–70), just off the Minories, part of a development designed by Dance the Younger. It is London's earliest crescent and was probably modelled on those of Bath.

Few churches were built in the City after Wren's, but some needed reconstruction in the 18th century. Of these, the most outstanding is St Mary Woolnoth (**22**), rebuilt under the provisions of the 1711 Church Rebuilding Act to replace a church damaged in the Fire. It is the work of Wren's most brilliant pupil, Nicholas Hawksmoor. The exterior, with twin towers fused to form a

broad and rather grim west entrance, is one of the most unforgettable in the City. The interior is equally striking: centralized and square, with clusters of Corinthian pillars supporting a dome. Butterfield fiddled with the interior in 1875, when the galleries were removed, but most of the excellent fittings remain, including the imposing reredos and bulbous pulpit. Occupying a very valuable site right in the heart of the City, the church has been threatened with demolition on several occasions, especially at the end of the last century when Bank underground station was constructed beneath it.

Other 18th-century churches in the City include All Hallows, London Wall, an early work by Dance the Younger. It has a charming interior, with a highly ornamental apse and barrel-vaulted roof lit by high semi-circular windows. St Botolph Bishopsgate (rebuilt 1727–9), and St Botolph Aldgate (1741–4) (**24**), both works of Dance the Elder, are also well worth visiting.

Since the readmission of the Jews to England in 1656 a Jewish community had become established in the City, and what is now the oldest place of Jewish worship in Britain, the Spanish and Portuguese Synagogue in Creechurch Place (known as Bevis Marks from the name of the street that runs past it), was built in 1700–1 to replace an earlier venue in adjacent Creechurch Lane. The architect was a Quaker, Joseph Avis, and he refused to take any fee from the congregation. The restrained classical style he employed is reminiscent of later 18th-century nonconformist chapels, but the many fine fittings create a sumptuous impression. Queen Anne donated one of the beams.

The mid-19th century was a time of transformation in the City, when it assumed its role as the world commercial centre that we know today. The

►26 Lothbury, which runs along the north side of the Bank of England. The spire belongs to Wren's St Margaret Lothbury (1686–90). In the foreground is no. 7, one of the best Victorian commercial buildings in London.

▼25 The Royal Exchange: the Cornhill façade of William Tite's building (1841–4). The competitions for its design were a fiasco. The first was declared null because all the designs exceeded the set estimates; the second was between Tite and C. R. Cockerell, the greatest architect of his generation – the other competitors withdrew so Cockerell would win; the commission was given to Tite, who had better connections in the City.

◄27 *Smithfield Meat Market. Trading starts at 5 a.m., the meat having arrived in the early morning, and business is mostly concluded by 8 a.m. By midday the market is deserted. The porters are traditionally known as bummarees.*

population gradually but steadily declined. In 1841 123,000 people were living there; by 1881 the number had dropped to 51,000. This was mainly because the growth of the City's commercial enterprises caused such a steep increase in the value of the land that most people could no longer afford to live on it. Land prices and rents have been rising ever since, and the City has been described as the most valuable piece of real estate in the world. Access to the suburbs, where most City workers now lived, became easier with the construction of railways. The first railway terminus in the City was Fenchurch Street Station (1841), and in 1863 the first underground railway in the world was opened – the Metropolitan Railway, from Paddington to Farringdon. Sharp increases in traffic led to the making of new roads, such as Queen Victoria Street, and the widening of others, such as Threadneedle Street.

The most sweeping aspect of the transformation was a great spate of rebuilding. It has been estimated that of every five buildings standing in the City in 1855 only one remained by 1901. Before Queen Victoria came to the throne in 1837, most businesses, including banking, were conducted in buildings domestic in both character and origin – often the town residence of the family who owned the business. Hoare's Bank (1829), in Fleet Street, still contains a family apartment.

The new monumental classical architecture was occasioned partly by a desire for prestige, but primarily by the sheer growth of trade and business which the old buildings were too small and inadequate to serve. During the early 19th century Britain had become the first industrialized nation in the world. Industrialization required finance, raised through such institutions as the Stock Exchange and the banks, whose activities correspondingly increased in size and sophistication. The City had always been important to the economic life of the nation, but its significance was now much greater. This trend was

▼ *28 Leadenhall Market, which is famous for its poultry and game (the shop displays at Christmastime are renowned), now also contains a great variety of other shops, open every weekday.*

accelerated and consolidated later in the century, when such innovations as the railways, the postal systems and electric telegraph all facilitated the centralization of business activities. Moreover, by the middle of the century Britain was at the centre of a vast and growing colonial empire yielding an increasing volume of trade. Much of the empire's produce was sold in the City's various commodity markets and exchanges, and thus the City's influence spread over the globe.

These developments led to new types and styles of building. Brick and stucco were no longer favoured, and architects abandoned the restraint of the Georgian manner; they built in stone, usually in richly Italianate classical styles. One of the earliest and grandest of these new structures still to survive is the Atlas Assurance Building, on the corner of King Street and Cheapside, designed in 1836 by Thomas Hopper. Gothic was less favoured in the City, but there is an outstanding example, the highly original no. 7 Lothbury (formerly the Auction Mart Company), designed by G. Somers Clark in a Venetian Gothic idiom (**26**). The Victorian City was at its grandest in Lombard Street. Sadly, little remains, apart from the City Offices Building (1868) at the corner with Gracechurch Street. This was the first of a new type of building in the City: it was designed to consist solely of lettable office space – in modern terms, an 'office block'. Though not one of the most distinguished buildings of its time, it displays many of the characteristic features of 19th-century City office architecture, notably a lavish use of ornament. The most interesting bank building surviving from this period is probably the National Provincial (now National Westminster) Bank in Bishopsgate (1865), designed by John Gibson. It is a single storey, with Corinthian columns running its full height, topped by statues, some of which represent towns served by the bank, including London, Manchester and Birmingham. The imposing banking hall is lit by three domes supported on red marble pillars.

Iron was increasingly used in the construction of buildings; one of the most interesting examples is nos. 59–61 Mark Lane, by George Aitchison – essentially an iron structure with stone used only as a cladding. Inside is a self-supporting iron staircase. The many warehouses erected at this time range from utilitarian buildings along the wharves to those that also comprised offices and showrooms, such as nos. 23–25 Eastcheap, built duing the 1860s by John Young for spice merchants. Also in Eastcheap, at nos. 33–35, is the eccentric vinegar warehouse, designed by R. L. Roumieu, with an elaborate Gothic façade.

One important old-established aspect of the City's commercial life has not yet been mentioned: its markets. Three of them were given new buildings in the 19th century, all designed by the City Architect, Horace Jones. The first was Smithfield, on a site which had been used for tournaments, fairs and a market for many centuries – the famous Bartholomew Fair was held here every year until 1855. Smithfield Market was originally for live meat: cattle were brought to be sold and slaughtered. The presence of the butchers' shambles (slaughterhouses) and the driving of herds through the narrow streets made the area increasingly insanitary, and intolerable for residents. It was vividly described by Dickens in *Oliver Twist* (1837–9): 'The ground was covered, nearly ankle-deep, with filth and mire; and a thick steam, perpetually rising from the reeking bodies of the cattle, and mingling with the fog . . . hung heavily above.' In 1852 the cattle market was moved to Copenhagen Fields, Islington; the building

▶29 *Petticoat Lane. Every Sunday morning, while the City lies silent and deserted, thousands of Londoners and tourists can be found heading towards its eastern boundaries, to this lively and bustling street market. Although officially renamed Middlesex Street during the 19th century, the street is still popularly known by its old name, which derives from the area's long association with the trade in cloth and clothes, especially old clothes. Today all kinds of merchandise can be found here and in nearby streets into which the market has spilled.*

of the central meat market at Smithfield in 1866–7 was precipitated by the railways' revolutionary effect on transport. Meat could now be brought to central London from all parts of the country. The other crucial new factor was refrigeration: in 1876 the first shipment of frozen meat arrived from America. Jones's building for Smithfield Market is still used for selling meat (**27**). It has a red brick façade, stone-domed octagonal towers on each of the four corners and impressive gateways. The interior has arcades of iron and glass, with stalls set on either side of a wide central avenue.

Leadenhall, named after the 14th-century lead-roofed mansion of Sir Hugh Neville that once stood nearby, has also been the site of a market for many centuries. Jones's attractive two-storied glass and iron building, which used to be famous chiefly for its game and poultry stalls, now houses shops selling all kinds of goods, and is a favourite lunch-time haunt of many City workers (**28**). The third market Jones designed, Billingsgate, is now incorporated into a new development. The fish market which it contained was moved in 1982 to a new site in Tower Hamlets – outside the City boundaries, as is Spitalfields fruit and vegetable market, but both are still administered by the City Corporation.

The 20th century has seen great changes in the City, notably in its physical appearance. The bombs of World War II left 225 of its 675 acres devastated. Several of Wren's churches were among the saddest losses, but St Paul's survived, although it received two direct hits. Its escape was largely owing to the efforts of the St Paul's Watch, a group which guarded the building against fire every night for the whole duration of the war. St Paul's became a symbol of hope to all British people but especially to Londoners, and few who lived through the Blitz will forget the sight of the magnificent dome surrounded on all sides by smoke and flames.

The devastation provided an opportunity, as in 1666, to rebuild the City

◄ 30 *The National Westminster Tower. The City's tallest building rises to a height of 600 feet (183 metres). Opened in 1981, its 52 floors provide office accommodation for about 2500 people.*

imaginatively – an opportunity that was partly wasted in the 1960s and early 1970s, when many indifferent tower blocks ended St Paul's long dominance of the City skyline. However, in some cases the result has been more heartening, with original and inventive structures. One of the best post-war buildings in the City is the P&O and Commercial Union Building, Leadenhall Street, designed by Gollins, Melvin, Ward and Partners (1964–9) and clearly inspired by the cool perfection of work by Mies van der Rohe (whose own design for a City tower block was never built).

Not all 19th-century buildings have been swept away by development schemes; conservationists are at work in the City. In some cases new buildings have been planned to accommodate the old. When the City's tallest building was constructed, the 600-foot-high tower for the National Westminster Bank (183 metres) (**30**), the old National Provincial Bank building (see above, p. 44) was retained in front of it.

The incessant building activity reflects the economic vitality of the modern City. Britain has lost her empire and other financial centres have become established in the world, but adaptation to changed circumstances has preserved the importance of the City in the international financial network, and it remains the world leader in its combination of financial and insurance services. Its vital role in the economic equilibrium of the nation is undiminished: its annual foreign income now exceeds £3000 million, double that of the British manufacturing industries.

The most ambitious building scheme has been the Barbican development (**31–3**), constructed on 62 acres in the north of the City that had been totally

▼ 31 *The Barbican. The architects of this very ambitious development have provided numerous contrasts of scale. There are soaring concrete towers, office blocks (**32**, overleaf) and a variety of smaller buildings. This long residential terrace is one of several, some grouped attractively around a lake and others surrounding a garden.*

33 *The Museum of London, on the south-west corner of the Barbican development. The building, by Powell and Moya and Partners, is skilfully arranged around two courtyards. Officially opened by the Queen in 1976, the Museum has won considerable critical acclaim. Its collections trace the chronological development of the capital through objects, models and vivid reconstructions, such as a very popular audio-visual representation of the Great Fire of 1666.*

◀ **32** *Barbican office block.*

laid waste in 1940. The idea of a single redevelopment project, first mooted in 1957, was taken up by the City Corporation partly as a means of attracting residents back to the City (by the 1950s the population had fallen below 5000). Besides housing, the site incorporates a vast arts centre, a school and, on the south side, an office development, London Wall. The architects were Chamberlin, Powell and Bon. The scheme took many years to complete and caused much controversy, its cost escalating beyond all expectation. Accommodation is provided in three great tower blocks, with balconies that give them a bristly appearance from a distance. Shakespeare Tower, 420 feet (128 metres), is one of the tallest residential buildings in Europe. The towers and the low-rise blocks of the rest of the Barbican are grouped around lakes and lawns; high walkways separate pedestrians from the traffic below. The 16th-century church of St Giles Cripplegate, where Milton is buried and Oliver Cromwell was married, the only old building incorporated in the complex, has been restored. The arts centre, the last part to be completed, was opened by the Queen in 1982. It includes two theatres for the Royal Shakespeare Company, a concert hall which provides a permanent home for the London Symphony Orchestra, an art gallery, a library and a cinema.

In the south-west corner of the Barbican is the Museum of London, covering the history of the whole of London, in a much-admired building by Powell and Moya (**33**). The collection is excellently laid out, illustrating by means of objects, models and reconstructions the development of London from prehistory to the present. For those who want to find out more about the history of the City of London, there is no better place to start.

Aspects of the City

The government of the City

The City's governing body is the Corporation. It is responsible for the running of the area, just like any other Local Authority elsewhere in Britain, but it also has unique powers and duties. These include running its own police force and Port Health Authority and maintaining four bridges over the River Thames (see below, p. 91). The policy-making body of the Corporation is the Court of Common Council. It consists of Common Councilmen and Aldermen, elected on non-political grounds to represent the 25 wards into which the City is divided for administrative purposes. To qualify to vote in their election one must either be a resident in the City or the owner or tenant of a property there with an annual gross value of at least £10. Each ward has one Alderman, who is elected to serve until he reaches the age of 70, and a number of Common Councilmen proportionate to its size (the Council has 130 in all), elected annually.

To serve as an Alderman or Common Councilman it is necessary to be a freeman of the City. Freemen are the citizens of the City, and until the 19th century only freemen were allowed to trade or practise a craft within the City boundaries. Being a freeman also used to entail other privileges, such as the right to vote at ward elections, immunity from tolls at markets and fairs, and the right, if convicted of a capital offence, to choose one's method of execution. Today the privileges are few (they include the right of admission to the Corporation Almshouse, a home for retired freemen), but the rank is still a highly valued honour. There are four ways of becoming a freeman: most commonly, by right of patrimony – descent from a freeman; by redemption – officially described as 'the purchase with the approval of the Courts of Aldermen or Common Council'; by servitude – apprenticeship to a freeman; and by presentation – an honorary gift of membership, usually only bestowed on statesmen and other individuals for exceptional service. The Queen, Robert Runcie, Archbishop of Canterbury, and the former Prime Minister Harold Wilson are all honorary freemen.

The Aldermen also form the Court of Aldermen, whose responsibilities include the administration of justice within the City and the final choice of the new Lord Mayor. The Lord Mayor is the chief citizen in the City, ranking second only to the sovereign. The post is an ancient one, originating in the years 1189–92; the first incumbent was Henry FitzAilwin who, contrary to later practice, held it for over 20 years. In 1215, in order to win favour with the citizens of London, King John granted a royal charter, still preserved in the Guildhall, which gave them the right to choose for themselves a Mayor each year, although their choice had to receive royal assent. The Mayor had con-

◀**34** *Temple Bar. The boundary between the Cities of London and Westminster at the western end of Fleet Street has been marked since at least the 13th century. The present monument (1880) was designed by Sir Horace Jones, the City Architect. It incorporates statues of Queen Victoria and the Prince of Wales by Boehm and is topped by a splendid griffin, the City's symbol. This monument replaces one by Wren, removed in 1878 to Theobalds Park, Hertfordshire, because it was an obstacle to traffic. In the background are the Royal Courts of Justice (1874–82), a masterly composition by G. E. Street.*

siderable power, not only in the government of the City but also in national affairs, and his help and support were often sought by influential groups. He was present at the signing of Magna Carta in 1215; he played an important part in the Peasants' Revolt of 1381 (Wat Tyler was killed by the Mayor); he was one of the leading signatories on the petition asking William of Orange to become king of England in place of his father-in-law James II in 1688. One of the City's most famous Mayors was Richard ('Dick') Whittington, whose story has been popularized in Christmas pantomime. He may have owned a cat, but he was certainly no pauper. A wealthy mercer, four times Lord Mayor of London, he died in 1423 leaving a multitude of bequests for the benefit of the City. The title 'Lord Mayor' was first used during the 15th century, but did not come into general and regular use until about 1500.

The election of the new Lord Mayor takes place on Michaelmas Day, 29 September, with much traditional ceremony and ritual. On this occasion (and on several others during the year) the reigning Lord Mayor and other officials carry nosegays of sweet-smelling flowers; in days gone by these protected the bearer against the stench of the streets and, it was thought, against infection. The Court of Aldermen selects the new Mayor from candidates (usually two) nominated by the senior members of the City livery companies. The result, however, is almost always a foregone conclusion, as the choice has been made a few years in advance. Apart from wealth – for certain expenses, including some banquets, have to be met from personal funds – the attributes of the new Lord Mayor must include long service with the City Corporation as both an Alderman and Sheriff, and membership of a livery company. The office of Sheriff is

▼ **35** *The Lord Mayor's Show. The procession sets out from the Mansion House, and travels down Poultry and Cheapside, past St Paul's, and then along Ludgate Hill and Fleet Street; it returns along the Embankment and Queen Victoria Street. The lavishly decorated Lord Mayor's coach, built in 1757, incorporates panels painted with allegorical scenes by the Italian artist Cipriani. It is accompanied by Pikemen and Musketeers of the Honourable Artillery Company. This regiment, one of the oldest in Britain (its origins can be traced back to 1537), has long and close links with the City, and always provides the Lord Mayor's bodyguard.*

36 *The Lord Mayor's Banquet, held at the Guildhall on the Monday after the Lord Mayor's Show. It is a splendid occasion attended by many leading City figures and by the Lord Chancellor, as head of the judiciary, the Archbishop of Canterbury, representing the Church, and the Prime Minister, who traditionally makes an important policy speech. The new Lord Mayor also makes a speech, in which he outlines the themes he intends to follow during his year of office. In this picture the Lord Mayor is making his speech; on his left are the Prime Minister, Margaret Thatcher, and the former Archbishop of Canterbury Dr Donald Coggan.*

the oldest in the City – it is first recorded in Anglo-Saxon times; and the City's right to elect two Sheriffs annually was granted by King John in 1199. The election is made by senior members of the livery companies on Midsummer Day, 24 June. The Sheriff's duties include attending meetings of the Courts of Common Council and Aldermen, attending sessions of the Central Criminal Court and executing certain writs of the court, and attending the Lord Mayor on official occasions.

The Lord Mayor's duties are also very varied and range from presiding over many meetings, including that of the Common Council, and attending justice sessions as Chief Magistrate in the City, to acting as host to numerous visitors, including heads of state, and travelling abroad as a representative of the City. To be Lord Mayor is still to occupy a powerful position, not least because throughout his year of office the Mayor meets a multitude of influential people, to whom he can put forward the views of the City on important issues. In September 1983 the first female Lord Mayor was elected, Lady Donaldson, who had previously been the first woman to be elected to the Court of Common Council and the first female Sheriff.

The second Friday in November is Admission Day, when the new Lord Mayor is sworn in at the Guildhall, taking up the symbols of office – the sword, mace, crystal sceptre, seal and 16th-century city purse – from his predecessor in a ceremony known as the Silent Change, as no words are spoken. The Lord Mayor is always preceded on ceremonial occasions by these symbols of office. On the day after Admission Day (the second Saturday in November) the Lord

Mayor's Show is held. This is a day of much pageantry and colour, and it also has a serious purpose, for the new Lord Mayor rides through the City to the Royal Courts of Justice in the Strand to be sworn in as Chief Magistrate of the City by the Justices of the Queen's Bench – a reminder of the days when all new Mayors had to be approved by the monarch. During the 15th century the procession became more and more elaborate; between 1422 and 1856 it took place on the river, and much of the spectacle was provided by the livery companies. After a period of decline in the 18th and 19th centuries, the Lord Mayor's Show has once again returned to popularity and splendour. The Lord Mayor rides in his magnificent 18th-century red and gold state coach, drawn by six great grey shire horses, escorted by a company of pikemen and musketeers of the Honourable Artillery Company (**35**). The procession includes numerous decorated floats, all depicting some aspect of the City and based on a central theme chosen by the Lord Mayor. On the Monday after the Lord Mayor's Show the Lord Mayor's Banquet is held at the Guildhall, a tradition dating back to 1501. It is a splendid affair and usually numbers the Prime Minister among the many distinguished guests (**36**). Other banquets and receptions are held during the year at the Lord Mayor's official residence, Mansion House.

The livery companies

Today there are 96 livery companies, of which several have come into being in this century, but the majority are hundreds of years old. The forerunners of the livery companies were the guilds, which originated in Saxon times: associations

▶38 *Stationers' Hall. The Stationers' Company, founded in 1403 and incorporated in 1557, has had a hall on this site since 1606. The present building was constructed after the Great Fire. Until the passing of the Copyright Act in 1911 every work published in Great Britain had to be registered here. A plane tree in the court behind the hall marks the place where formerly all books condemned by Church and State authorities were burned.*

▼37 *Skinners' Hall courtyard. The quiet 17th-century courtyard of Skinners' Hall, Dowgate Hill, is reminiscent more of Italy than of London.*

of men, usually sharing a common trade, grouped around a local church whose saint they adopted as their patron. At first they were largely religious fraternities, concerned with the well-being of members in life and the saying of Masses for their souls after death. Gradually each guild began to take control of its members' particular craft; some sought official recognition for this move from the start, while others were fined by Henry II in 1179 for not requesting royal assent.

Over the next 200 years the guilds won many privileges from the monarch, often in return for financial support. These rights were embodied in charters (the first recorded charter was granted to the Weavers in 1184) which confirmed various powers, such as the power of search (the right to inspect all goods produced and handled by members) and the control of wages and prices. These powers strengthened the guilds' grip on the City's trade and furthered their prosperity. The granting of livery status to guilds (involving the right to wear a distinctive costume) began in the reign of Edward III and remained a royal prerogative until the 16th century, when it was transferred to the City. Two ancient companies have never received livery status, the Parish Clerks and the Watermen and Lightermen. As in the past, each company is presided over by a Master and three or four Wardens, elected annually.

There was intense rivalry between the major guilds, on several occasions breaking out into violence. One of the most contentious subjects was the order of precedence. This was finally fixed by the Lord Mayor and the Court of Aldermen in 1515 and still obtains, reflecting the relative strength and importance of the companies at that date. The first five, in order of precedence, are the Mercers (dealers in luxury fabrics), Grocers, Drapers, Fishmongers and Goldsmiths. The Skinners and the Merchant Taylors, bitter rivals, took it in turns each year to be numbers six and seven – the origin of the phrase 'at sixes and sevens'.

The 15th and 16th centuries saw the heyday of the livery companies: their influence over the City's trade was at its zenith and their ritual and ceremony were at their most splendid. The major guilds often tried to outdo each other in displays of wealth and pomp on festive days, when royalty visited the City or during the Lord Mayor's Procession or the Midsummer Marching Watch. This last was traditionally a muster of able-bodied men, who paraded with arms through the City streets. Over the years it developed into an increasingly elaborate and costly spectacle until Henry VIII prohibited it in 1539. The Goldsmiths were renowned for the four-towered castle they set up in Cheapside on such occasions, with wine flowing from two sides of it. Feasts were also an important part of company life, and were sometimes very lavish. When the Merchant Taylors entertained James I and his son Prince Henry in 1607 they spent over £1000, a vast sum in those days. Entertainment is still an important aspect of the companies' activities; although dinners are not as elaborate as they often used to be, several old traditions are still maintained. At some company dinners, for example, the guests drink from a loving cup, often an old and valuable piece of silver. Mindful that in the 10th century King Edmund the Martyr was stabbed in the back while drinking a cup of wine, each guest protects his neighbour by standing back to back with him. At a dinner held by the Clothworkers' Company, the guests are likely to be asked whether they dine with Alderman or Lady Cooper. Depending upon their reply, they will be given either brandy or gin to drink. This custom is said to have originated in the 17th

century, when Alderman Cooper died after attending a dinner at the Clothworkers' Hall; his wife blamed the strength of the brandy for his sudden demise, and provided funds to ensure that in future gin would be offered as an alternative.

During the Civil War most of the companies supported the Parliamentary cause, often with large sums of money – which was mostly never repaid. The companies suffered during the Plague, when trade in the City was brought to a standstill; in the Great Fire nearly every one lost its hall, and some lost their records as well. Although they gradually recovered their financial position and rebuilt their halls, they never regained economic supremacy, and the City was henceforth dominated by the Bank of England and the newly emergent great trading associations.

Although their continued relevance and usefulness has been questioned, especially in the latter years of the 19th century, the livery companies have survived and indeed flourish with added strength. Those who have joined their ranks in the 20th century include the Master Mariners, Launderers and Chartered Accountants. Many of the wealthy companies continue, as in the past, to devote much of their substantial income to charitable purposes. Several famous schools, such as Merchant Taylors, Oundle (the Grocers) and Tonbridge (the Skinners) were founded by liverymen individually or as a company; the schools maintain links with their founders. The companies also sponsor awards and professorships at various universities and continue to support almshouses for old members of the company and their widows. Some, such as the Goldsmiths and Apothecaries, are still closely involved with their trade, while others have adopted modern trades, now that their original crafts are obsolete: the Fanmakers have interests in the ventilation and heating trade, while the Horners, once engaged in making articles of horn, are involved with the plastics industry.

Many companies still have a hall, where members and their guests can be entertained and company business transacted. The first companies known to have possessed halls were the Merchant Taylors and Goldsmiths in the 14th century, but neither theirs nor other companies' original halls remain; the few survivors of the Great Fire were destroyed, along with many reconstructed halls, during the Blitz. The Apothecaries' Hall, on a quiet courtyard in Blackfriars Lane, escaped bomb damage. It was built in 1684 and altered in the 18th century. Inside, the Court Room, Library and Great Hall have their original magnificent 17th-century panelling. The Skinners' Hall in Dowgate Hill (**37**) also dates from the 17th century, with a façade much remodelled in the late 18th century. As their financial position improved in the 19th century, many of the companies rebuilt their halls. Among the best is the Goldsmiths' Hall, a very handsome Italian palazzo style building in Foster Lane (**43**); designed by Philip Hardwick in 1835, it has a sumptuous interior. In the Court Room is a 2nd-century Roman altar to Diana, found in 1830 on the site of the building. The Goldsmiths also possess some interesting portraits and, not surprisingly, a huge and extremely fine collection of plate. The Fishmongers' Hall was rebuilt in 1834, the third hall on this site (the second one had to be demolished to make way for the new London Bridge); it was badly damaged during the war, and has been carefully restored. Henry Roberts, assisted by the young George Gilbert Scott, was responsible for the design, one of the finest and purest examples of the early 19th-century Greek revival. To take advantage of the magnificent site, overlooking the river, all the principal rooms are located on the first floor.

Many of the companies that had to rebuild their halls after World War II incorporated several floors of lettable office space as well as the hall in their new building – for example, the Plaisterers, whose new hall in London Wall was opened by the Lord Mayor in 1972. As well as their halls, some companies own very valuable property in the City; the Carpenters and Dyers between them own Throgmorton Avenue, and St Helen's Place belongs to the Leathersellers. In many cases such property was bequeathed to them centuries ago and now makes a major contribution to their continuing wealth.

City ceremonies

Although much of the physical evidence of London's history has disappeared, striking remnants of the past are preserved in the ceremonies that occur throughout the year, not all as spectacular or well known as the Lord Mayor's Show. Most have a serious purpose behind them, but many are simply quaint reminders of another age.

Among the best known and oldest is the Ceremony of the Quit Rents, which takes place every October. On this occasion the City's legal officer, the City Solicitor, pays the Queen's Remembrancer (an officer responsible for the collection of debts due to the sovereign) 'quit', or token, rents for two ancient properties, the forge in St Clement Danes and the Moors in Shropshire. The exact location of the Moors is not certain; it may be the Moor House estate at Alveley near Bridgnorth. The rent for the forge is six horseshoes and 61 nails, while that for the Moors, once two knives, one sharp and one 'so weak it would bend in a new cheese', is now a billhook and a hatchet (the significance of these symbols has been forgotten). The ceremony takes place at the Law Courts in the Strand.

Two of the City's famous writers are commemorated each year in separate services. One for the diarist Samuel Pepys is held on or near 26 May at St Olave's, Hart Street, where Pepys and his long-suffering wife, Elizabeth, are buried. During the service, which is attended by the Master and Wardens of the Clothworkers Company (Pepys was a Master Clothworker in 1677) and the Elder Brethren of Trinity House (of which Pepys was appointed Master in 1676), the Lord Mayor places a wreath of laurel leaves in front of the communion rails, and an address is given, usually by a renowned Pepys authority. A service in memory of John Stow, author of *The Survey of London* (1598), takes place at his parish church of St Andrew Undershaft on or near 5 April. His monument in the church shows him seated at his desk, quill in hand; during the service the Lord Mayor changes the quill for a new one.

The annual presentation of the Knollys rose to the Lord Mayor is a custom revived in the 1920s. Traditionally, the rose represents a fine imposed on Lady Constance Knollys in the 14th century for building a bridge across Seething Lane without permission; however, records show that permission had been granted – the rose is an acknowledgement of this and not a fine. Nowadays the rose is taken from the Port of London Authority Garden in Seething Lane and carried to Mansion House by the churchwardens of All Hallows, Barking.

Every year the Lord Mayor also receives a boar's head on a silver platter, presented by the Butchers' Company. This is again a modern revival, of a ceremony dating back to the 13th century, when the butchers were granted a piece of land where they could 'cleanse the entrails of beasts'; in return they

▶ 44 Child's Bank, no. 1 Fleet Street, designed by John Gibson in 1879. Founded in 1671 by a goldsmith named Wheeler, and continued by his son-in-law, Francis Child, this is one of the oldest banks in the country; today it is part of Williams and Glyn's. The bank was built on the site of the Marigold Tavern, and Gibson used stylised marigolds to decorate the entrance to his building. The Royal Courts of Justice, on the opposite side of Fleet Street, can be seen reflected in the window. Gibson designed numerous banks throughout the country in inventive classical styles; he was the architect of the National Westminster building in Bishopsgate (1865).

gave the Mayor a boar's head. Another annual ceremony connected with the activities of the livery companies, also dating from the 13th century, is the 'Trial of the Pyx', which takes place every February or March at Goldsmiths' Hall, when members of the Goldsmiths' Company test the weight and accuracy of the coins of the realm minted during the previous year. One coin for every 5000 minted is placed in a sealed box (the pyx); these are checked for weight and metal content. Nowadays there is little to be gained from making lightweight coins or debasing metal, but in earlier centuries it was a lucrative crime, and those found guilty used to be severely punished, sometimes having their hands cut off.

A long-standing tradition still performed by some companies is the meeting of members on their company's saint's day to elect their Warden and other officials for the coming year and then to walk in procession, wearing their livery, to attend a service in their church. The procession of the Vintners' Company is always led by one of their wine porters, dressed in a white smock and top hat, carrying a brush to sweep the road – a reminder of the days when the streets were full of filth. In 1612 John Norton left a bequest to the Stationers' Company for the preaching of a sermon in the Chapel of St Faith in the crypt of St Paul's (now the Chapel of the Order of the British Empire) on Ash Wednesday, to be followed by the distribution of cakes and ale to members of the company. The Stationers have continued to fulfil his wishes.

The financial City

Activities in the City today focus so strongly on the world of finance that to many people the term 'the City' is virtually synonymous with finance. Despite the relative weakness of the British economy in recent years and the fall of sterling against other world currencies, the City of London has managed to remain one of the most powerful financial centres in the world, largely because it provides an immense variety of banking and monetary services and offers a system that has proved adaptable to successive changes over the years. Business in the City is concentrated in such a small physical area that it is easy to build up personal contacts, enhancing that element of trust which is so important in financial dealings and is embodied in the famous motto of the Stock Exchange – 'My word is my bond'.

Banking

Banking lies at the heart of the financial system. The first people we know of as bankers were the goldsmiths of the Middle Ages; they bought bullion both on their own account and for their customers and then issued 'notes' in respect of it, the right to the bullion passing with the note as it changed hands. But it was not until the end of the 17th century that banking became a business in its own right. One of the first banks still exists, Child's, at no. 1 Fleet Street (**44**) (now amalgamated with one of the clearing banks, Williams and Glyn's). Its early ledgers include details of the account of Charles II's mistress Nell Gwynne. Today, as a stroll down Lombard Street (**45**) or Bishopsgate soon reveals, the City contains hundreds of banks. The Bank of England stands alone as a unique monolithic institution; the other banks fall into the categories of clearing banks, merchant banks and, in growing numbers in the 1970s and 1980s, foreign, especially American, banks.

The Bank of England

The idea of a national bank was put forward on several occasions during the 17th century. Demand for one became especially strong in 1640 when Charles I sequestered £200,000 which merchants had deposited with the Royal Mint for safekeeping, and again in 1672 when Charles II took a forced loan from the Exchequer, where many had stored their funds. It was not, however, an idea that secured the support of the government until 1694, when, desperately in need of funds to finance its war against the Dutch, it granted a charter to the Bank of England in return for a loan of £1.2 million, which was raised by public subscription. Initially the Bank was little different from the goldsmiths' and other banks that were springing up in the City and throughout the country, but it did have the advantage of being a bank of issue (i.e. it had the right to print banknotes) as well as being a bank of deposit. Moreover, the privileges it gained over the years from various Acts of Parliament had important long-term effects, especially as it gained a monopoly of note issue in England in 1844 (although it was not until 1921 that the last bank also to have a right of issue, Fox, Fowler & Co., disappeared).

The Bank of England also gradually emerged as the banker's bank. It took on a certain responsibility for the action of others by its occasional intervention during a crisis and by being the repository for other banks' balance of cash. It is also the government's bank, in that it holds the account of the Exchequer and borrows on its behalf in the money market through the issue of Treasury Bills.

For most of its history the Bank was a privately owned joint-stock company operating under a royal charter. In 1946 it was nationalized; in spite of sombre warnings, this has made little change in practice, at least as far as the City is concerned. The Bank is run by a governing body known as the Court, which meets every Thursday. It consists of the Governor, a powerful figure in the nation's monetary affairs, the Deputy Governor and 16 directors, all appointed by the Crown (i.e. the Prime Minister).

Initially the Bank had no home of its own and operated from Grocers' Hall, but in 1724 it acquired its present site in Threadneedle Street, where the Bank's surveyor, George Sampson, erected a Palladian-style house for it. The Bank's familiar soubriquet, 'The Old Lady of Threadneedle Street', is probably derived from a cartoon by Gillray (1797) depicting an elderly lady (the Bank) trying to prevent the Prime Minister, Pitt the Younger, from seizing her gold. Sampson's house was replaced between 1788 and 1808 by a highly original building designed by Sir John Soane. This was a single-storey structure, surrounded by a windowless screen wall; its five banking halls with their characteristically Soanian shallow domed ceilings were lit by a series of internal courtyards. Today hardly anything of Soane's work survives, for pressure of space caused the Bank to commission Sir Herbert Baker to design a new and vastly bigger building in the 1920s – an architectural tragedy (**47**). Soane's screen wall survives more or less intact on the Threadneedle Street and Prince's Street frontages, but the rest of the Bank, which now rises to seven stories, was completely rebuilt, as were Soane's subtle and beautiful interiors, of which some details were unhappily imitated by Baker. Even this extension did not prove sufficient to cope with expanding business and in 1953 some of the Bank's departments moved to a rather dull building in Cheapside.

The Bank's vaults still house the nation's gold reserves, so security is of paramount importance. After the Bank was attacked during the Gordon Riots

of 1780, a detachment of the Foot Guards of the Household Brigade, known as the Bank Piquet, marched to the Bank every evening and remained on watch throughout the night. This practice was discontinued only in 1973, when an electronic alarm system was installed. Doormen at the Bank of England wear a distinctive uniform, with pink tailcoat, red waistcoat and gold-trimmed top hat.

The clearing banks

Retail banks were set up in great numbers throughout the country in the 18th and 19th centuries. Their main function, like that of their successors, was to hold deposits and make loans. From small and local beginnings, they grew through amalgamation and the opening of new branches, and rapidly emerged as a new financial force which soon became involved with the City. Today four giants dominate this world – Lloyds, Barclays, National Westminster and the Midland – but little more than a hundred years ago there were over 300 retail banks. Of these, 200 were joint-stock banks, owned by their shareholders, and the rest private banks, owned by an individual or a family.

The 'big four', as they are often known, all have their head offices in the City and maintain close links with the Bank of England. The bulk of the banks' transactions are by means of cheque. Each day millions of cheques are cleared in the Clearing House in Post Office Court, Lombard Street, which has been in existence since 1833. Before then the clerks from each bank had to go to other banks to present cheques for payment and then return to their own with the cash. To make life easier for themselves, the clerks took to meeting to exchange their cheques, so that they needed to carry only cash equivalent to the balance

▲47 *The Bank of England lies at the heart of the City, on the junction of most of its main streets. When the Bank was rebuilt (1921–37), the screen wall of the old building, by Soane, was retained. The Bank now rises seven storeys above the street and has three basement storeys. The statue of the Duke of Wellington is by Francis Chantrey (1844).*

of the difference between the cheques drawn on each bank. Initially, the Clearing House, where the clerks met, was run by the private banks; the joint-stock banks were not allowed to participate until 1854. Today there are two main clearings of cheques every day – 'town' (London) and 'general' (the rest of the country) – both done by computer. While they are best known for their high-street banking, in recent years the major clearing banks have extended their activities to advising their clients on tax, estate duty and general investment problems. The 'big four' have also set up their own merchant banks to deal with the area known as corporate finance, advising on and implementing the more sophisticated company acquisitions and mergers. They have branches and offices in many countries throughout the world.

Merchant banks

Merchant banks are rather difficult to categorize. Their name is somewhat misleading, as today they are rarely merchants and need not even be banks (although most are). Although most of them are now companies, and some even public companies, the majority tend to retain strong links with the families who set them up. Despite being in many ways peculiarly British institutions, many are foreign in origin: in the 19th century London's reputation as a trading and banking centre drew many important foreign financial families, such as the Rothschilds and Barings, to the City. They saw the financing of trade as a logical extension of their other activities, for the money they had earned gave them the ability to back others. This often involved the guaranteeing or 'accepting' of bills of exchange, and today the elite of the merchant banks are known as the 'Accepting Houses'. There are usually around 16 or 17; an Accepting House loses its status if it is taken over by a foreign bank, for it is laid down that as well as being of the highest financial standing and based in the City, the Accepting Houses must be British controlled. Other merchant banks are known as Issuing Houses.

Throughout the 19th century the merchant banks were primarily concerned with financing international trade and arranging loans on the British market on behalf of foreign countries. It has been estimated that of the £3600 million lent by Britain to overseas countries between 1870 and 1914, about 40% was provided by the merchant banks. In the early 1980s the banks became less sanguine about such ventures, but they have continued to diversify. Their activities include corporate finance, advising industrial and commercial concerns on raising capital, dealing in foreign currencies, managing pension funds, and advising individual clients on personal investments.

The discount market

The Discount Houses play a vital role in the short-term money market. They make their living by borrowing money from financial institutions, especially clearing banks, which have cash to spare and need to invest it for a short period. They invest these funds in various paper assets, such as commercial bills or Treasury Bills (issued each week by the Bank of England on behalf of the government), buying them at a little below their face value. They then either sell them at a profit or keep them until they become repayable. As the funds that they borrow are repayable on demand or at very short notice, it can happen that the Discount Houses do not have sufficient sums to cover themselves at a given moment; in that case they have the right to go for funds to the Bank of England, in its capacity as lender of the last resort. The Discount Houses always charge a slightly higher rate than they pay the banks from which they borrow; this small difference can create substantial profits for them, for they have an enormous turnover.

The commodity markets

Today, as for over 200 years, the London commodity markets play an essential role in the international marketing of the world's produce, for they link producer and consumer. In the 18th century they were centred on the Royal Exchange, where those concerned with a particular commodity would gather under one arcade (or 'walk') to do business. As foreign trade increased and London became one of the world's busiest ports the Exchange proved too small and the merchants began to congregate in the various coffee-houses that had sprung up since the end of the 17th century. Soon some markets, such as the Wool Exchange, had their own buildings, as did the the sales conducted by the East India Company. In those days nearly all sales were conducted by auction; today this usually happens only in the case of tea, furs and ivory. The bulk of sales are now conducted by private treaty arranged by the commodity brokers, who earn commission for the services they render to both buyer and seller. The majority of goods no longer come to London to be stored in warehouses prior to their sale, but are transferred direct from producer to consumer.

Central premises for the sale of commodities that did not have a specific market of their own were first established in 1811 at the London Commercial Sale Rooms in Mincing Lane. The building was destroyed in 1941 and the

▼**48** *Rothschilds' Bank: the headquarters of one of the best-known names in the City, the merchant bankers Rothschild and Sons. This handsome building, arranged around a courtyard and faced with black polished granite, is in St Swithin's Lane. It was designed by H. Fitzroy Robinson and Partners and built in 1963–5. The Rothschilds have been in England since the end of the 18th century. They opened their first Accepting House (merchant bank) in the City in 1809.*

markets moved to Plantation House, home of the Rubber Exchange, which became the London Commodity Exchange. Pressure of space forced another move, to the former Corn Exchange, Seething Lane, in the 1970s. The Commodity Exchange is now run by a board of directors, but they have no control over the methods and conditions of trading in the various markets, which operate under the rules of their own association.

So-called 'futures markets' provide an insurance for commodity users by allowing them to hedge against changes in the prices of raw materials. Such markets can be set up only in commodities that can be accurately described by grade or quality – coffee, cocoa or vegetable oils, for instance; the goods can then be traded in lots of a given weight for future delivery at an agreed price. In 1983 a new practice was introduced, of dealing in futures in foreign exchange rates (known as LIFFE).

The Baltic Exchange

The Baltic Exchange is a good example of a great City institution arising from the most informal beginnings. In the 18th century merchants with an interest in trade with northern Europe and Russia congregated in the Virginia and Maryland coffee-house, Threadneedle Street, which consequently changed its name to the Virginia and Baltic. Today the Baltic is the world's major international shipping exchange. Its members find ships for cargo and *vice versa*; it has been calculated that about 75% of all the world's open market bulk cargo movement is at some stage handled by the Baltic. Its other activities include the buying and selling of ships for clients, a grain futures market and the potato futures market. In recent years the chartering of air cargo space has proved an increasingly large part of business.

Since 1903 the Baltic has been housed in a grand Edwardian building in St Mary Axe. This has an impressive trading floor of over 20,000 square feet (1857 square metres) and marble columns and walls. The floor is divided informally among the various sections of the market, and here the representatives of the approximately 700 companies that make up the Baltic Exchange are entitled to trade. As in many City institutions, all business is done verbally. In the middle of the floor is a rostrum where a 'waiter' (so called in deference to coffee-house days) calls out the names of members whom their firms or clients wish to contact.

The London Metal Exchange and the Gold Market

In the 18th and early 19th centuries the metal market was mainly domestic. It was conducted at first in coffee-houses, particularly the Jerusalem, in Fleece Passage, Cornhill. But technical changes and economic growth made London the major clearing house for the world's surplus metal by the mid-19th century. In 1877 the London Metal Exchange was formed with the primary aim of providing a protective mechanism for the producers, merchants and users of metal by fixing a price before delivery, thus shielding them against price fluctuations which can occur through economic or political disruptions. This only became possible with the development of the telegraphic cable, which was used to receive notice of metal shipments. Three months was the approximate time it took ships to reach London from the producing countries in the late 19th century, and contracts are still traded for the delivery of the metal within a three-month period.

49–51 *Bank signs. Until the end of the 18th century the City's streets were full of hanging signs, for in the days when most people were illiterate, and streets had no numbers, they were the best means of identifying business premises. But they were also a hazard to traffic and most were removed early in the 19th century, though some, such as these bank signs, remain. The king's head (above) belongs to the Royal Bank of Scotland; the sign of the black horse (below) hangs outside Lloyds Bank offices. The gilded grasshopper (centre) was the emblem of Sir Thomas Gresham, founder of the Royal Exchange, who lived in a house on this site. It was adopted by Martin's Bank, now part of Barclays.*

Trading is conducted by 'open outcry': contracts result from bids and offers shouted across an open floor, 'the Ring'. Formerly the brokers stood around a chalk ring drawn on the floor when making their offers; now they sit on benches arranged in a circle. They call out the amount they wish to buy or sell at a given price for delivery on a particular day. There are two trading sessions daily, one in the morning and one in the afternoon, and each metal traded on the Exchange is dealt with in each session in two five-minute dealings. The official prices for the day are usually the closing prices of the second dealing ('ring') of the morning session; they have to be agreed by the Quotation Committee before being announced by the Secretary of the Exchange. On the basis of these prices the majority of long-term domestic and international contracts are concluded. This is the only market in the world that trades internationally in the seven most important non-ferrous metals – copper, zinc, tin, lead, silver, aluminium and nickel.

Gold is dealt with differently; its price is still fixed twice daily in the 'fixing room' of N. M. Rothschild, one of the City's five bullion houses (dealers in gold). One dealer from each house sits at a desk with a small Union Jack in front of him, which he raises or lowers to indicate whether or not he is willing to deal at a given price; when sales and purchases are balanced, the price is declared 'fixed' and immediately transmitted around the world.

The Stock Exchange

The Stock Exchange is essentially a market place for company, Local Authority and government securities. It is also important as a place where capital can be raised for new businesses. Dealers in stocks and shares first met at the Royal Exchange, and by the 18th century they had become established in their own 'walk', but the uproar they made was so unpopular with other traders in the Exchange that they were forced to move into an open street, Exchange Alley. The alley contained a coffee-house, Jonathan's, that many of them began to frequent and use as a place of business. They soon felt the need for a more formal system and place of trading, and in 1773 they moved to their own building, known as 'New Jonathan's'; the Stock Exchange had come into being.

In 1802 a formal constitution was drawn up. With the decline of the Amsterdam Bourse and the rapid industrialization of 19th-century England, the London Stock Exchange became the world's leading stock market, a position it retained until 1914. In turnover of business it now ranks third, after New York and Tokyo. It is run by a council of elected members which lays down strict rules concerning the quotation of dealings in securities and punishes those who infringe its rules. So far it has managed to stave off any significant interference by the government in its affairs.

Business on the Stock Exchange is at present conducted by brokers and jobbers, each having a clearly defined role: the brokers buy and sell shares on the instructions of their clients, earning money on commission, while the jobbers buy and sell shares on their own account, making money by the amount of profitable trading that they do. Jobbers usually specialize in a particular type of security. Members of the public are not allowed to deal directly with them, but must approach them through the brokers. The price of shares is not fixed by the jobbers but fluctuates according to supply and demand, and can be significantly influenced by the political and economic situation at home and abroad.

On the floor of the Stock Exchange, where business is conducted, numerous

hexagonal stands are grouped around the room according to sections of the market; these are occupied by the jobbers, while the brokers hurry around between the stands searching for the best deal (brokers and jobbers can be distinguished by the different coloured badges that they wear in their lapels). The floor, which can be viewed from the visitors' gallery, is the scene of ceaseless activity, with large groups milling around the stands, phoning their offices, or watching the *Financial Times* Index of share prices, which is electronically displayed on the wall (**52**). Although women have been admitted to the floor since 1973, it is still a very male preserve.

At the beginning of the 1980s the Office of Fair Trading was examining Stock Exchange procedures to see if they fell within the province of the Restrictive Practices Act. In 1983 a vote in Parliament determined, to the City's relief, that the Stock Exchange should be left to put its own house in order. However, it imposed three provisos: the abolition, by 1986, of minimum commissions (the minimum – and generally accepted – percentage charge on a deal made to a customer); the ending of single capacity (the distinction between jobbers and brokers); and the extension of permissible investment by outside concerns (both foreign and British) in Stock Exchange firms to a maximum 29.9% share. The abolition of the minimum commission will benefit the more efficient and in general the larger firms, and will accelerate the growing tendency to increased professionalism in forecasting market trends. The extension of the outsider's permissible stake has attracted strong interest from foreign investors and, at home, from large institutional investors and the clearing banks.

The Stock Exchange now inhabits an enormous modern building which replaced the spacious glass-domed Victorian Exchange in 1973. It is dominated by a 26-storey polygonal tower, 320 feet (97.5 metres) high.

▲**52** *The floor of the Stock Exchange. The frenetic activity of the Stock Exchange can be observed from the public viewing gallery. The jobbers operate from the hexagonal stands and the brokers move between them, searching for the best prices for their clients.*

Lloyd's and insurance

One of the best-known City institutions is Lloyd's of London, the most important insurance concern in the world. In the late 17th century men seeking insurance cover for their ships went to those London coffee-houses in which underwriters congregated and in particular to that of Edward Lloyd, who started business in Tower Street in about 1686. He moved to Lombard Street in 1691. Lloyd was not an underwriter himself, but he took an interest in the business, seeing it as a means of increasing his trade: he sent runners to the docks to obtain the latest information about the arrival and departure of ships and published a regular bulletin and a shipping list. These were the forerunners of *Lloyd's List*, first printed in 1734 and still published by the firm. It provides general shipping news and information about the arrivals and departures of merchant ships throughout the world, as well as details of marine and aircraft casualties.

To avoid those whose interest in insurance was of a gambling nature, the serious underwriters moved premises and set up their own committee. In 1774 they took rooms in the Royal Exchange, which remained their home until 1928. The organization ceased to be called a coffee-house only in 1844. Increased membership has caused Lloyd's to find several new premises. In 1928 it moved to a building in Leadenhall Street designed by Sir Edwin Cooper, and in the following decades purchases of adjoining properties made it one of the largest landowners in the City. A large extension in Lime Street, designed by Terence Heysham (1950–7), is connected to the original building by a bridge. A further extension, designed by Richard Rogers, architect of the Pompidou Centre in Paris, promises to be an exciting and controversial addition to the City's modern buildings.

Lloyd's was initially concerned mainly with marine insurance, and it now

▼53 *Commuters hurrying to work across London Bridge. Nearly half a million pour into the City every weekday. The traditional 'City gent', dressed in a dark three-piece suit and bowler hat, with a furled umbrella and a copy of the 'Financial Times' under his arm, is becoming increasingly rare: dress is now more informal (although suits remain de rigueur).*

also underwrites large aviation, commercial and industrial risks, for example providing compensation for a firm trading in the Third World that loses its assets by being nationalized. It avoids the purely speculative, but is not afraid of the extraordinary: Marlene Dietrich's legs were insured with Lloyd's, and a whisky company which had offered a prize to the person who caught the Loch Ness Monster insured against the possibility of anyone's doing so (the underwriters stipulated that any creature captured must be brought to London for identification by a qualified zoologist).

Lloyd's is not a company, but a corporation. This means that individual members are personally responsible for paying out on claims. To spread this financial liability, members, known as 'names', are grouped into syndicates which operate collectively. There are around 20,000 members grouped in about 400 broking and underwriting syndicates. Individual members have to have readily realizable capital of at least £100,000. The corporation was established by Act of Parliament in 1871 and the constitution there laid down has changed little, although after a series of scandals in the 1970s outside representation – including nominees of the Bank of England – has been introduced onto the committee that is responsible for the day-to-day administration.

The Underwriting Room, usually known simply as 'the Room', where business is transacted, is a vast marbled-lined hall. It contains pew-like desks called 'boxes', set in rows. Syndicates rent box space according to their size. A member of the public cannot deal directly with underwriters but must approach them through a broker, whose job it is to find the best offer for his client and then prepare a policy. This policy must then be approved by the Lloyd's policy signings agency. Employees of the corporation, like those of the Baltic Exchange, are known as 'waiters' and wear livery, a reminder of Lloyd's coffeehouse beginnings.

The famous Lutine Bell, which hangs in the Underwriting Room, was salvaged from a French frigate, *La Lutine*, which sank in 1793 with a highly valuable cargo of bullion that Lloyd's had underwritten. Contrary to popular belief, the bell is rung before any announcement of importance and not just to tell of the loss of a ship. It is struck twice for good news and once for bad.

Besides the international business transacted at Lloyd's, a large proportion of British life and general insurance is handled in the City. Insurance is the biggest employer in the City and forms one of the largest elements in its invisible earnings, for now more business is done abroad than at home. One of the earliest forms of insurance in which the City specialized was against fire. This became important in the late 17th century, in part because the City had recently been so badly ravaged by fire. The pioneer was Nicholas Barbon, who founded a company called the Insurance Office for Houses in 1681 and soon had many emulators. All the early companies had their own fire engines, and identified the buildings they covered by fixing distinguishing plaques on them; these were known as fire marks, and they can still be seen on some 18th-century City houses.

The College of Arms

The College of Arms was first established in what is now Upper Thames Street by Richard III to provide a home for the heralds. It was the heralds who arranged the tournaments which were such an important feature of medieval

▶ **54** *The College of Arms, the home of the heralds, built 1671–88. The porch is surmounted by the royal coat of arms with the arms of the college below. The building seems to have been designed by Maurice Emmett Junior, master bricklayer to the Office of Works, working with Francis Sandford, Lancaster Herald. The interior contains some excellent 17th-century woodwork.*

courtly life. At the tournaments they accompanied the knights to the joust, kept the scores and proclaimed the victors. They were often retained by the monarch and great nobles as members of their households. Henry VII, however, cancelled their charter of incorporation and gave their home to his mother; they were re-established by Queen Mary in 1555 and presented with the mansion of the earls of Derby, on the site of their present home.

Today the College consists of the thirteen heralds of England, Ireland and Wales, presided over by the Earl Marshal, the Duke of Norfolk. The chief herald is known as the Garter King of Arms; he is supported by Clarenceux (who has jurisdiction as grantee of armorial bearings south of the River Trent) and Norroy (whose jurisdiction is north of the Trent to the Scottish border), six other heralds and four pursuivants (junior or probationary heralds). All are appointed by the sovereign after nomination by the Earl Marshal. Their main work is, as it has always been, tracing and recording pedigrees, establishing the right to bear arms, and similar matters of genealogy and precedent. They also help to organize state ceremonies, at which they often appear. The College will on request, for a fee, investigate anybody's right to bear arms.

The home of the College of Arms (**54**) was built during the 1670s by Maurice Emmett, a master bricklayer to the Office of Works. It now forms three sides of a courtyard; the fourth side was lost when Queen Victoria Street was driven in front of it. The fine gates and railings round the building were melted down during World War II, and in 1956 an American, Mr Blevis Davis, presented the College with the present splendid (probably 18th-century) gates and railings from the recently demolished Goodrich Court in Herefordshire. The library contains the world's finest collection of heraldic and genealogical material.

Fleet Street

Fleet Street is named after the River Fleet, which once ran south from Hampstead to meet the Thames just west of Blackfriars Bridge. Until the 13th century it was a tidal river and boats could travel up it as far as Holborn. Later it became blocked with refuse and complaints about its smell began, but no improvement was made until the 17th century when the river was straightened – a project supervised by Wren and Hooke – and made into a canal with broad wharves. It was never much used and the refuse was soon as bad as before. Finally in 1766 'that stinking abomination', as it was called at the time, was cased in.

Fleet Street, now famous as the home of the English newspaper industry, is part of the highway that links the Cities of London and Westminster. The boundary between them, at the western end of Fleet Street, was once marked by Temple Bar, an imposing gateway designed by Wren. This was moved in 1878 to Theobald's Park, Hertfordshire, as it was proving an obstacle to traffic, and was replaced by the present memorial, which is topped by a griffin, the City's emblem (**34**).

Printers preceded journalists in Fleet Street: Wynkyn de Worde, assistant to Caxton, moved here in about 1500, after his master's death, and Richard Pynson, printer to Henry VIII, also worked in the area. The earliest English daily newspaper, the *Daily Courant*, a single sheet reporting overseas news, was started in Fleet Street in 1702, the first of many national and provincial newspapers to have made their home here (it ran until 1735). In recent times

►**55** *The Daily Express Building. The stylish headquarters of Express Newspapers (1931) is easily the most exciting and individual building in Fleet Street; it was designed by Ellis and Clarke with Sir Owen Williams. The exterior is entirely covered with black and transparent glass set in chromium strips.*

some of the large national newspapers have moved out, although most have not gone far; *The Times*, once nearby in Printing House Square, is now just outside the City in Gray's Inn Road, while the Mirror group of newspapers has a large new building in Holborn. Many others remain, including the *Daily Express*, housed in a stylish black glass and chromium building of 1931 (**55**). The foyer is decorated in black, gold and silver: a quintessentially thirties interior. Next door is the *Daily Telegraph* building, only four years earlier, but much more conventional. On the opposite side of the street are Reuters (the international press agency) and the Press Association, housed in one building of 1935 designed by Lutyens. The *Sun* and *News of the World* have their headquarters in Bouverie Street, one of the best places to visit late at night to capture the atmosphere of speed and excitement as the morning papers go to press and are then rushed away to be distributed throughout the country.

This is an area rich in pubs and cafés, some well known, like El Vino's, renowned as a haunt of journalists and for its long resistance to women buying drinks at the bar. There has been an inn on the site of the Olde Cheshire Cheese in Wine Office Court since at least 1538; the present building was put up after the Great Fire, in 1667 (**57**). It has many literary associations. In the 1890s it was the regular meeting-place of the circle of poets known as the Rhymers' Club, which included W. B. Yeats. In the 18th century it was reputedly often visited by Dr Johnson. His fine late 17th-century house, 17 Gough Square (**56**), in one of the many alleys and courts that lead off Fleet Street, was his home between 1749 and 1759, and here he compiled his famous *Dictionary of the English Language* (1755). The house is now a museum containing material relating to the life of Johnson and his circle. Other writers associated with the area include

◀**56** *Dr Johnson's House. 17 Gough Square, a handsome late 17th-century house, was the home of Dr Johnson between 1749 and 1759. Here he and six assistants compiled his famous 'Dictionary of the English Language' (1755). Today the house, which is open to the public, has been restored as far as possible to its original state.*

57 *The Olde Cheshire Cheese, Wine Office Court. This well-known City pub lies close to the heart of Fleet Street. It is a favourite of journalists and has long-standing literary associations. There has been a tavern on this site since the 16th century; the present building was erected in 1667, immediately after the Great Fire.*

Samuel Richardson, author of *Pamela* and *Clarissa*, early masterpieces of the novel. Richardson had a printing press in Blue Bell Court, where one of his employees was the novelist, playwright and poet Oliver Goldsmith, who had lodgings in the Temple. Charles Lamb, a later inhabitant, met such friends as Coleridge, Keats and Wordsworth in the local coffee-houses, which were subsequently frequented by Dickens and Thackeray.

To the south of Fleet Street lay an area known as Alsatia, which from the Reformation to the end of the 17th century was a notorious haunt of rogues and vagabonds. It was centred around the former Whitefriars Priory, whose ground was a legal place of sanctuary until 1697, providing its inhabitants with a refuge from justice. The most famous denizen of the underworld here was Mary Frith, better known as Moll Cutpurse, whom Dekker and Middleton made the central figure of their play *The Roaring Girl* (1610). She was both a thief and a forger and often dressed in men's clothes and smoked a pipe – behaviour which her contemporaries found even more fascinating than her crimes.

St Bride's, often called 'the journalists' church', is just off the eastern end of Fleet Street. Excavations have revealed that there has been a church here since the 6th century and before that there was a Roman building (a small piece of mosaic floor can be seen in the crypt). In the Middle Ages this was one of the four City churches from which the curfew was rung at 9 p.m., indicating that it was time for the City gates and taverns to be closed. It was here that Samuel Pepys, who was born nearby, and his eight brothers and sisters, were baptized. The church was destroyed in the Great Fire and rebuilt by Wren. It is best known for its steeple, Wren's tallest (it was shortened after being hit by lightning in 1764) and, for some, his most beautiful, with five diminishing octagonal stages. The traditional tiered wedding cake is a replica of this steeple, which was first copied by a local baker in the 18th century. All the church apart from the steeple was destroyed in 1940; it has been restored, but the interior (**58**) is not an exact replica of Wren's work. In the crypt is a permanent exhibition of the history of the church and its neighbourhood. Inside the church are the figures of a boy and girl from a former charity school in Bride Lane and a memorial to Virginia Dare, the first English girl to be born in America (1587), whose parents were married in this church.

The other church in Fleet Street is St Dunstan-in-the-West, which was rebuilt in 1829 by John Shaw. Its most remarkable feature is a tower with an open octagonal lantern at the top, modelled on All Saints Pavement, York. The clock, with effigies that strike the bells, was set up in 1671, and is thought to have been the first clock in London with minute divisions. The statue of Elizabeth I on the exterior probably dates from 1586; it comes from the Ludgate, a demolished City gate. In the vestry are three other statues from the Ludgate, believed to represent the mythical King Lud and his two sons (see above, p. 7).

▶58 St Bride's, Fleet Street, designed by Wren (1671–8), is a fine example of the sensitive restoration of a City church gutted in World War II. The modern fittings are in Wren's style. This view, looking west, shows a sculpture of St Paul by David McFall (it is matched opposite by one of St Bride). At the east end is an oak reredos carved in the style of Grinling Gibbons.

Legal London

The Temple

'The Temple' is the name given to the strip of land between Fleet Street and the river which houses the two Inns of Court that have their home in the City, Inner Temple and Middle Temple. Inns of Court (there are four altogether; the other two are Gray's Inn and Lincoln's Inn) train and accommodate barristers – lawyers who practise as advocates in the High Court.

The Temple takes its name from the Order of the Knights Templar, a company of knights created in the early 12th century and established throughout Europe to safeguard the pilgrim routes to Jerusalem. They were called 'Templars' because their arms were kept in a convent on the site of Solomon's temple. The Temple had become their London home by 1162 and here they built their church, which still survives. The wealth and power of the knights made them politically undesirable and the entire European Order was eventually suppressed after confessions of blasphemous activities had been extorted from its members by torture. The English Order was dissolved by Edward II in 1321 and the Temple was given to the Knights Hospitaller. They in turn rented the land to a group of lawyers and their students, who styled themselves 'the Society of the Temple'. The Society was divided into two, Inner and Middle Temple, during Henry VI's reign. ('Inner' and 'Middle' refer to the inns' proximity to the City; there was once an inn called the 'Outer Temple', but it never housed lawyers: an 'inn' was simply a hostel.) Henry VIII confiscated the Hospitallers' lands, but the lawyers were allowed to remain as tenants and in 1608 the Benchers (governing body) of the Inner and Middle Temple secured the freehold of the land from James I.

The oldest building in the Temple is Temple Church, now the joint chapel of the two societies. The earliest part, the nave (**59**), was built for the Knights Templar between 1160 and 1185; its circular form is modelled on the Church of the Holy Sepulchre, in the tradition of the Order's churches. Architecturally it

◀ **59** *Temple Church: the circular nave (1160–85), one of the earliest Gothic buildings in England. On the floor are the remains of a famous series of monuments to 12th- and 13th-century knights, which was badly damaged by an incendiary bomb in May 1941.*

is important as an example of the transition from the Norman style to the Gothic; some of its features are still essentially Norman, for instance, the west door and round-headed aisle windows, but the arches of the main arcade are pointed. They are built of Purbeck marble – the earliest surviving architectural use of this material in London. Between the blank arches on the aisle walls are carved grotesque heads, said to represent souls in heaven and hell. Early in the 13th century the church was enlarged by the addition of a rectangular chancel, which has three vaulted aisles of equal height separated by Purbeck marble arcades of great beauty. The chancel was carefully restored after bomb damage and the reredos of 1682, made under Wren's supervision, which had been removed by the Victorians, was replaced. There is some good modern stained glass by Carl Edwards; the east window shows the Blitz, with St Paul's surrounded by flames. In the north-west corner of the choir are the slit windows of the 'penitential cell', a chamber less than 5 feet (1.5 metres) long, where knights who broke the rules of the Order are said to have been imprisoned. One, Walter le Bacheler, is reputed to have starved to death here.

The layout of the Temple dates from the 17th century. Its informal groups of buildings of various periods arranged around inter-connecting courts give it the feel of a large college at Oxford or Cambridge; it is always peaceful, even though the noise of Fleet Street is so close. Few of its 17th-century buildings have survived 19th-century rebuilding and 20th-century bomb damage. Among those which have remained largely untouched are the 17th- and 18th-century houses of King's Bench Walk (two attributed to Wren), which have mellow brick façades. Many badly damaged buildings have been rebuilt as almost

▼ **60** *Middle Temple Hall (1562–70), the dining hall of one of the four Inns of Court. It is usually open to the public in the mornings. The lamp hanging in the arch is lit, like all lamps in the Temple, by gas. They are the last public gas-lamps in London, and are lit each evening by a lamplighter.*

exact copies of the originals, the Master's House, just to the east of Temple Church, being a good example.

The Temple's chief architectural glory, after the church, is Middle Temple Hall (1562–70) (**60**). The interior is spanned by a splendid double hammer-beam roof. The panelled walls are decorated with portraits, armour and the arms of members of the inn; some of the heraldic glass in the windows is 16th-century. The screen is a magnificent piece of Elizabethan oak carving. The serving table is said to be made of timbers from Drake's ship *The Golden Hind*, and the high table, where the Benchers eat, was a gift from Elizabeth I. In the 16th and 17th centuries the Inns of Court were famous for the masques, plays and other entertainments mounted in their halls; there is a tradition that Shakespeare's *Twelfth Night* was first performed in Middle Temple Hall in 1601. Inner Temple Hall was completely destroyed during World War II and rebuilt in a soothing neo-Georgian style.

The boundaries between the Inner and Middle Temples are not very apparent but their buildings can be distinguished by the devices they bear: the *agnus dei* (lamb and flag) for Middle Temple and a winged horse for Inner Temple. The Temple's gardens stretch down to the river. This is the setting of the famous scene in Shakespeare's *Henry VI Part 1* in which rival Yorkists and Lancastrians pluck the white and red roses which are to be their emblems in the ensuing Wars of the Roses.

The Inns of Court still have the exclusive right to admit barristers to the profession. Students, who are all law graduates, no longer have to live in an inn, but they must 'keep terms', which in effect means eating a specified number of dinners in the hall of their inn, and must pass an examination taken after a year's study at the Council of Legal Education in Gray's Inn. Successful candidates are 'called to the bar', admitted as barrister in a ceremony held by their inn. Then, after a year's pupillage to a practising barrister, they compete for admission to a set of barristers' chambers, almost all of which are situated in the Inns of Court. Only if they find a place in chambers can they practise. The income of the inns is largely derived from the rents paid by barristers' chambers, and some of it is used to provide scholarships and prizes to help students struggling to establish themselves at the bar.

The Old Bailey

The Central Criminal Court, or 'Old Bailey' as it is always known, was erected on the site of Newgate Prison in 1902. Designed by Edward Montford in an elaborate neo-Baroque style, it has a copper dome surmounted by a bronze statue of Justice, 12 feet (3.5 metres) high, who carries the sword and scales in her outstretched arms but, contrary to popular belief, is not blindfolded. Over the main entrance are the sculpted figures of Truth, Patience and the Recording Angel, with the inscription 'Protect the Children of the Poor and Punish the Wrongdoer'. Inside there is a very grand marble entrance hall. The Lord Mayor, as the City's Chief Magistrate, often attends the opening of the quarterly sessions here; the central chair on each bench (panel of judges) is always left empty if the Lord Mayor is not present. There are 23 courts, the most important trials being held in courts numbers 1 and 2. If the case is particularly sensational, large queues form up outside for the limited amount of public viewing space.

The City police

The City still maintains its own police force, the only one in the country not under the direct control of the Home Secretary. It has been in existence since the 18th century, though it was not formally recognized as a separate body until 1839. The force is fairly large for the area it covers – but then this is no ordinary area. Nowhere else in England are so many banks and other important financial institutions concentrated into a small area where 400,000 people come to work every day, creating special problems of security and policing. City policemen can be distinguished by their crested helmets and gold buttons.

The Tower of London

One of the principle decisions of William the Conqueror after his victory at Hastings in 1066 was to build castles throughout England to ensure his control over his new kingdom. Beside England's largest town he built the most important castle: the Tower of London. Originally the Tower lay entirely within the Roman city walls, but its enlargement extended it eastwards, and now it lies in the borough of Tower Hamlets. The central keep, the White Tower (**61, 62**), was begun in 1077 and was finished during the reign of the Conqueror's son, William Rufus. Building was supervised by Gundulf, Bishop of Rochester. Constructed of Caen stone specially imported from France, it is the largest tower of its type apart from that at Colchester, and remains one of the finest examples of military architecture in the country – a castle, a palace and a symbol of the sovereign's might. During the Middle Ages it was whitewashed, hence its name. Structurally it has been little altered since Norman times; an extra floor was added to the interior in 1600 and the windows were enlarged by Wren early in the 18th century.

At first William's fortress was surrounded only by a defensive ditch, but gradually a curtain wall and various bastion towers were added. These were

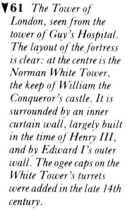

▼**61** *The Tower of London, seen from the tower of Guy's Hospital. The layout of the fortress is clear: at the centre is the Norman White Tower, the keep of William the Conqueror's castle. It is surrounded by an inner curtain wall, largely built in the time of Henry III, and by Edward I's outer wall. The ogee caps on the White Tower's turrets were added in the late 14th century.*

begun by Richard I, but the bulk of the work was carried out in the reigns of Henry III and Edward I. Edward also began a second curtain wall, with its own bastions (**63**). Today the Tower is basically a keep surrounded by a double ring of walls and towers, with various buildings in the intervening spaces. From the late 13th century the whole complex was ringed by a moat (fed by the Thames), which was drained in 1843 and subsequently became a parade ground.

One of the earliest parts of the inner wall is the late 12th-century Bell Tower, one of the first examples in England of a polygonal wall tower. Here the future Queen Elizabeth was kept during much of the reign of her sister Mary. Later towers include the Wakefield Tower, where some of the royal apartments were situated, and the Salt and Devereux Towers, all built by Henry III. Most prominent of all is Edward I's Beauchamp Tower (*c*. 1300). It takes its name from Thomas Beauchamp, Earl of Warwick, who was a prisoner here in the late 14th century. He was followed by many other prisoners, some of whom carved their names on the walls. 'IANE', which can be seen here, is said to have been carved by Robert Dudley, husband of the tragic Lady Jane Grey, queen for nine days. Both were imprisoned in the Tower, and both were executed here in 1553. The only surviving original gateway to the inner ward is the Bloody Tower, known before the late 16th century as the Garden Tower. It is reputedly the place where 'the Princes in the Tower', the young sons of Edward IV, were murdered.

The landward entrances of Edward I's outer wall, the Middle and Byward Towers, remain, although altered. A portcullis with its winch is preserved in the Byward Tower, together with an early 14th-century wall painting of Christ in Majesty, which has been uncovered in the main room over the gatehouse. The late 13th-century St Thomas's Tower, once the river entrance, is better known as Traitors' Gate, for here condemned prisoners arrived by boat to await their execution.

The Tower also contains some impressive ecclesiastical architecture. The Chapel of St John, on the second floor of the White Tower, is a very fine example of early Norman building. Its tunnel-vaulted nave and gallery and groin-vaulted aisles are austerely simple: there is no carved decoration apart from some plain Tau crosses on some of the capitals. The chapel was used by the sovereign throughout the Middle Ages, and was on at least one occasion the scene of great drama – when Simon Sudbury, Archbishop of Canterbury, was dragged from his prayers to a bloody execution by rebels during the Peasants' Revolt (1381). After the Tower had ceased to be a royal residence the chapel was neglected and during the reign of Charles II it became the storehouse for state records. It was restored to its proper use in 1857, thanks to the intervention of Prince Albert.

St Peter ad Vincula was originally a parish church, but by the mid-13th century the expansion of the Tower had brought it within the castle precincts. It was burnt down and rebuilt in the early 16th century, and its roof of chestnut wood dates from this time. The magnificent 15th-century tomb of John Holland, the Duke of Exeter, was originally in the church of St Katherine-by-the-Tower, now demolished. Those interred in St Peter include Sir Thomas More, Anne Boleyn, Lady Jane Grey and the Duke of Monmouth, who had all been beheaded on Tower Green, outside the church: the site of the block is marked with a plaque. Private execution such as they were accorded was the privilege of only the most distinguished prisoners.

► **62** *The White Tower, the central keep of the Tower of London, was built between 1077 and 1097 under the direction of Gundulf, Bishop of Rochester. It is one of the finest examples of Norman military architecture in the country. Constructed of stone specially imported from France, its walls are 12 feet (3.5 metres) thick at the base. The windows were remodelled by Wren early in the 18th century.*

Though the Tower was built as a fortified royal palace, not as a prison (contrary to popular assumption), it has like most castles been used from its earliest times to house important men detained by those in power. The first recorded prisoner was Ranulf Flambard in 1100, who also had the distinction of being the first man known to have escaped from the Tower – he used a rope smuggled to him in a pot of wine. But it was not until the 15th century, and the dynastic struggles of the Wars of the Roses, that the Tower began to acquire its reputation as a place of intrigue, deep dungeons and murderous deeds. Henry VI died here in mysterious circumstances and here the Duke of Clarence was, according to tradition, drowned in a vat of Malmsey wine. The Tower's most famous victims were the Princes in the Tower, Edward V and his younger brother. How they met their fate is unknown; their uncle, Richard III, is the most likely villain, but he has his stout defenders. Henry VIII was the monarch who made most use of the Tower as a prison: during his reign the French ambassador declared that 'when a man is prisoner in the Tower none dare meddle with his affairs, unless to speak ill of him, for fear of being suspected of the same crime'. Two of Henry's wives, Anne Boleyn and Catherine Howard, several of his ministers and numbers of his subjects were imprisoned here. Some were executed or tortured – the rack (which stretched its victims) and the 'Scavenger's daughter' (which squashed them) were the most popular devices – but this was the fate of the minority. Others were free to wander around the Tower precincts, have visits from their families (who in some cases lived in the Tower as well) and keep servants. Sir Walter Raleigh, who spent many years as a prisoner here before his execution in 1618, had his own library, wrote books,

▼**63** *The Tower of London. This cannon, on the wharf outside the Tower, is part of a battery captured by the Duke of Wellington at Waterloo. Behind are contrasting styles of Tower architecture: the grim stone river walls built at Edward I's orders, and the delightful half-timber work of the mid-16th-century Queen's House.*

and was allowed to conduct scientific experiments. Treatment of the prisoner depended on his wealth and rank, the nature of his crime and whether or not he managed to establish friendly relations with his gaolers.

During the 17th century the Tower began to be less used as a prison. Samuel Pepys was imprisoned for a short spell after the Popish Plot in 1679 (on a happier occasion he unsuccessfully dug for treasure in the Tower), and the Jacobite rebels of the 1715 and 1745 uprisings were held here. In 1747 one of their leaders, Lord Lovat, was the last man to be executed on Tower Hill (the site of public executions, now called Trinity Square). Lord Nithsdale, another rebel, was more lucky; in 1716 he escaped from the Tower dressed as a woman, in clothes smuggled in by his wife.

The 17th century was also the last period in which the Tower was used as a royal residence, Charles II being the last monarch to observe the custom of spending the night before his coronation here. It continued to be used as an arsenal and ordnance office until 1855. The Royal Mint, in the Tower from the mid-13th century, moved out in 1812 and was followed by the Records Office in 1851. In 1235 Henry III had begun a royal menagerie in the Tower, following the gift of three leopards from the Emperor Frederick II; this moved to Regents Park in 1834, to form the nucleus of the London Zoo. Its ravens, however, were left behind, for Charles II had been told that their departure would be followed by the collapse of the White Tower and the downfall of the kingdom. They disappeared of their own accord in 1946, but without apocalyptic consequences; they have since been reintroduced and as before are a favourite of visitors.

Today the Tower houses two important collections, the Crown Jewels and the Armoury. The Crown Jewels have been kept in the Tower for centuries; they were shown to the public in a very casual way until Captain Blood made his famous attempt to carry them off in 1671, after which measures were taken to display them more securely. They can be seen now in the specially constructed Jewel House in the west wing of the 19th-century Waterloo Barracks. Most of the Crown Jewels were either sold or melted down during the Civil War and Interregnum, so there is little that is earlier than the late 17th century. The oldest piece is an anointing spoon, which dates from the 12th century. The most spectacular item is probably the Imperial State Crown made for Queen Victoria; it is set with over 3000 jewels, including a ruby given to the Black Prince which was worn by Henry V at Agincourt and a huge diamond, 'the Star of Africa'.

The Armoury is one of the finest collections of armour and weapons in the world. It occupies almost the whole of the White Tower. Here can be seen several suits of armour that belonged to Henry VIII and the richly decorated armour of Charles I. There is also a suit just over 3 feet (1 metre) high, believed to have been worn by the court dwarf of Charles I's wife, Henrietta Maria.

Although the Tower has been in part a museum since the mid-18th century and is today the country's most popular tourist attraction, its military functions have never been discontinued. During both world wars it was used as a prison and spies were shot here in secret; its last prisoner was Rudolph Hess, incarcerated for a short time after his abortive attempt to make peace with Churchill in 1941.

The chief officer of the Tower is the Constable. This once powerful position dates back to the Tower's foundation. Since the late 18th century the Constable has always been a senior army officer; one of the most famous was the Duke of

Wellington, Constable from 1824 to 1852. Formerly the post was tenable for life, but since 1933 it has been a five-yearly appointment. When the Constable visits the Tower he stays in the 16th-century half-timbered Queen's House. The Yeoman Warders (**64**), or 'Beefeaters' as they are popularly known (a medieval expression meaning 'well-fed servants'), were created by Henry VII in 1485. Their duties were originally to guard the prisoners and attend the gates; they are still responsible for the security of the Tower and its visitors (and make formidably well-informed guides).

Every night for nearly 700 years the famous Ceremony of the Keys has taken place at the Tower. The Chief Yeoman Warder, accompanied by a group of soldiers from the Tower Guard, sets out from the Bloody Tower and locks in succession the Outer, Middle and Byward Gates. As the party returns to the archway of the Bloody Tower, the sentry cries 'Halt! Who goes there?' The Chief Yeoman Warder replies 'The keys.' 'Whose keys?' 'Queen Elizabeth's keys.' The sentry then allows the party to proceed. The keys are saluted by the Tower Guard and taken to the Resident Governor for safe-keeping overnight. The ceremony is usually concluded at 10 p.m. precisely.

Other traditions associated with the Tower include the Beating of the Bounds, which occurs every third Ascension Day, a reminder of the time when all parish boundaries were regularly perambulated to impress them on the minds of parishioners. A short service is held at St Peter ad Vincula before the procession sets out, led by the Chief Yeoman Warder, followed by local choir-boys, Tower children and the Tower chaplain. Each child is issued with a

▲**64** *Inspection of the Yeoman Warders ('Beefeaters') outside the Queen's House in the Tower of London. They are wearing their royal livery, a red tunic trimmed with gold and a white ruff, only worn on special occasions. The Yeoman Gaoler at the end of the line is carrying the axe which used to be carried beside prisoners going to and from their trials. If the prisoner was found guilty the blade of the axe was turned towards him. Today it is brought out only for ceremonial occasions, as is the mace, which is traditionally carried by the Chief Yeoman Warder.*

willow stick, and at each of the 31 parish boundary-marks the procession stops and the chaplain declares 'Cursed is he who removeth his neighbour's land-mark', whereupon the Chief Warder shouts 'Whack it boys, whack it!' and the children beat the mark with their sticks. When all the stones have been beaten the procession returns to the Tower and sings the National Anthem on Tower Green. A more gentle ceremony occurs annually on 21 May, the anniversary of the death of Henry VI in 1471. The Provosts of Eton and of King's College, Cambridge (both institutions founded by the king) lay a sheaf of white Eton lilies and one of red roses respectively on the spot where he is thought to have been murdered.

The River Thames

Only a very small fraction of the 215-mile-long River Thames actually flows through the City, but the river has been vitally important to its development as a trading, commercial and banking centre. Ever since the Romans built the first quays here, almost 2000 years ago, the Port of London has contributed to the City's growth and prosperity.

As the quantity of shipping using the port grew throughout the Middle Ages, the City acquired from the Crown, in return for financial and political support, various rights and privileges concerning the port's activities, such as the weigh-ing and packing of cargoes and the sorting of spices. Wool provided the City's earliest major source of wealth: it was England's most valuable export, and to ensure that the customs dues, on which royal finances closely depended, were efficiently collected, monarchs maintained 'the Staple', a market where wool for export was compulsorily collected, taxed and sold. The Port of London had the

▼65 *The Custom House: the river façade, seen from the tower of Guy's Hospital. There has been a building on this site serving a similar purpose since the late 14th century. One by Wren was destroyed by fire in 1718. Construction of the present building began in 1817 to the designs of David Laing; he was replaced in 1825 by Sir Robert Smirke, architect of the British Museum. In the Long Room, captains of newly arrived ships deliver a report of their cargo and describe any unusual events of the voyage. St Dunstan-in-the-East can be seen behind, to the left.*

right of 'scavage' – it supervised the packing of wool for the Staple. The City did not suffer when cloth replaced wool as the country's main export, for London was the English port used by most merchants, since it was convenient for the main cloth importing centres of Germany and the Low Countries.

Many foreign traders were attracted to the City and they brought important benefits in terms of contact with trading centres throughout the world, but their presence was often resented by English merchants. Among the longest established of these foreigners were the Hanseatic merchants, who first came to London in the 10th century. By the 12th century they had their headquarters at Dowgate, where they built a guildhall and warehouses known as 'the Steelyard' (a corruption of the German *Stapelhof*, a courtyard where goods could be displayed or sold). They were very successful, and native merchants, jealous of their privileges, secured their explusion from England in the 16th century. However, some German merchants later returned, and a warehouse on the site of the Steelyard was owned by the cities of Lübeck, Hamburg and Bremen until 1853, when it was pulled down for the building of Cannon Street Station.

By Elizabethan times about half of England's total customs revenue came from shipping using the Port of London. To ensure that none of this escaped, the Crown in 1558 designated 20 'legal quays', all between the Tower and London Bridge, as the only places where ships could lawfully discharge their cargoes. This eventually led to appalling congestion as the size of ships and volume of trade steadily increased throughout the succeeding centuries; some ships had to wait at least a week before entering the Pool of London (that part of the Thames just below London Bridge) and then another three or four before they could discharge. Yet it was not until the end of the 18th century that the government

▼**66** *Trinity House. This is the home (right) of the 'Guild, Fraternity and Brotherhood of the most Glorious and Undivided Trinity', a body incorporated by Henry VIII, which has responsibility for all light-houses, lightships and sea-marks in Britain; it is also the country's chief pilotage authority. The building (1793–5) by Samuel Wyatt was gutted in World War II, but the façade has been restored and new premises built behind. On the left is the former headquarters of the Port of London Authority, a massive and ornate building designed by Edwin Cooper 1912–22.*

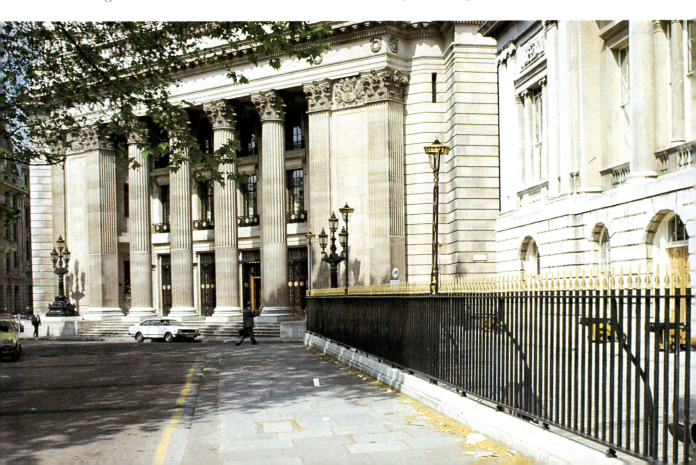

67 *St Katharine's Dock, perhaps the most attractive of London's docks, was designed by Thomas Telford. Built 1824–8, it covers 23 acres. In 1968 it ceased to operate commercially and its buildings were converted to new uses. Today it is a lively yachting centre and also houses the World Trade Centre in a reconstructed warehouse and a hotel and flats. In the East Dock is a fascinating collection of ships.*

permitted the extension of the docks. In 1799 the West India Dock Act was passed, authorizing the building of a new dock on the Isle of Dogs. This was soon followed by the Surrey Commercial Docks, the East India Docks and St Katharine's Dock, all beyond the City's boundaries. Because of the ever-increasing size of vessels these docks in turn have become obsolete, and the business of the Port of London is now concentrated on Tilbury. Many of the old docks lie deserted, their buildings derelict or demolished. The Greater London Council is eager to redevelop dockland and St Katharine's Dock has been converted into a sailing and leisure centre (**67**); a new World Trade Centre, a large hotel and several blocks of flats have been built there. In 1909 the Port of London Authority (**66**) was created to take over the running of the docks from the privately owned companies which had thitherto administered them; they no longer come within its jurisdiction, but it still has responsibility for the tidal areas of the river as far upstream as Teddington.

Nowadays there are relatively few vessels on the Thames, but for several centuries it was London's main highway. Many hundreds of watermen earned their living by taking people up or down stream or from one bank to the other. They often received a bonus for 'a barge beneath the bridge' – shooting the rapids between the piers of London Bridge, which was regarded as so dangerous that most passengers preferred to alight before reaching the bridge and walk to rejoin their craft on the other side.

The river was also the scene of much pageantry. The Lord Mayor, the monarch and many of the livery companies and great noblemen had magnificent painted barges with decorative awnings which they used on state occasions, such as the coronation of Anne Boleyn in 1533, when the procession to Westminster included over 50 barges. There were also festivities on the river during the famous Frost Fairs, held on occasions in the 17th and 18th centuries when the Thames froze over completely. Stalls were set up on the Thames, traders hawked their wares and even oxen were roasted on the ice. The last Frost Fair was in 1814; the removal of the old London Bridge increased the current and the building of the embankments made the river narrower and deeper, so the Thames has never frozen again.

Two traditional ceremonies take place on the river every year (both in July), Doggett's Coat and Badge Race and Swan Upping. The former is the oldest race still rowed on the Thames; it was first held in 1716, when the actor Thomas Doggett offered a prize of a coat and a badge for a race among Thames watermen to honour the accession of George I. Today it is rowed from Swan Steps to Cadogan Pier, Chelsea, against an ebb tide; it is open to six members of the Watermen's livery company who have completed their apprenticeship within the previous year, and the winner is presented with a red coat and a silver badge.

Swans have long been considered royal birds, and a Keeper of Swans is still employed as an official of the royal household. He presides over Swan Upping, which originated with the practice of monarchs allowing favoured noblemen to own a few swans. Only the Vintners' and Dyers' Companies retain this right on the Thames, and swanherds from the two companies, with the Keeper, round up cygnets between London Bridge and Henley. The cygnets are 'upped', marked on their beaks to distinguish their ownership. A single nick on the beak indicates that the bird belongs to the Dyers; two nicks, that it is the Vintners'; all unmarked swans belong to the Queen. This explains the traditional inn name 'Swan with Two Necks', a corruption of 'Swan with two nicks'.

It is usual to think of the river as murky and polluted, but it was once clean

▼68 *Tower Bridge: the familiar view of this famous bridge (1886–94). Its Gothic appearance was ordered by Parliament, who wanted it to harmonize with the Tower of London. On the right, moored on the south bank of the Thames, is HMS Belfast, the largest cruiser ever built for the Royal Navy. It was launched in 1938, took part in battles during World War II and opened the bombardment of Normandy on D-Day. Saved from the scrapyard in the 1960s, it is now open to the public.*

and full of fish. In the Middle Ages, City apprentices complained about the too frequent occurrence of Thames salmon in their meals. Improvements have been made recently and fish again swim in the Thames; even salmon have been caught.

City bridges

The City Corporation maintains, and when necessary rebuilds, the four bridges that cross the Thames from the City to Southwark: London Bridge, Tower Bridge, Blackfriars Bridge and Southwark Bridge. Money for this purpose comes from the income of a fund known as the Bridge House Estates, which has accumulated since the days when benefactors left money and property to 'God and Bridge' – to repair and maintain London Bridge, for long the only bridge to span the river at London.

The first reference to London Bridge dates from 1008, but this was probably not the first medieval bridge and it certainly replaced a Roman one (see above, p. 7). Made of wood, it suffered badly during various battles and had to be repaired several times: in 1097 a special tax was raised for the purpose. In 1176 work began on replacing it with one of the first stone bridges to be built in medieval Europe. This took 33 years to complete, and its construction was supervised by a priest, Peter of Colechurch, who died before it was finished. He was buried in the chapel that stood on the bridge together with rows of shops and houses flanking the rather narrow carriageway. The completed bridge was over 900 feet (274 metres) long and stood on 19 arches carried on piers surrounded by wooden platforms, with a central drawbridge. Though in need of constant repair, it remained the only bridge across the Thames downstream from Kingston until 1749. In 1758 the shops and houses were removed to make the roadway wider. It was eventually replaced in 1831 with a bridge designed by John Rennie, who also died before completion of the work. In 1971 a wider, stronger bridge was opened, spanning the river in just three broad arches and carrying six lanes of traffic. Rennie's bridge has, however, been preserved: it was purchased by an American oil company and reconstructed in Lake Havasu City, Arizona.

Tower Bridge (**68**), the lowest bridge on the Thames, is today one of London's most familiar and best-loved monuments, yet when it was begun in 1886, to the designs of Sir John Wolfe Barry and Sir Horace Jones, it was much criticized for spoiling a good view of the Tower. Parliament had decreed that the public should be allowed access across the bridge, so two walkways linking the bridge's towers and lifts to reach them were constructed. After being closed for many years (because, it was rumoured, of the number of suicides committed there) they are now open again. The two drawbridges of the central carriage-way are raised twice daily in summer to allow a paddle steamer service to pass through, and also on special occasions: they were raised in 1965, when Sir Winston Churchill's funeral cortège passed near the bridge, and in 1977, when the Queen's Silver Jubilee Progress passed under it.

The iron and steel structure of Blackfriars Bridge is an impressive example of Victorian engineering and craftsmanship, erected in 1865–9; it is the second bridge on this site. The first Southwark Bridge was built by a private company in 1815–19, also to the designs of Rennie, and was purchased by the City Corporation at the beginning of the 20th century. The present bridge was designed by Sir Ernest George and opened by George V in 1921.

Index

Numbers in *italic* refer to the key of the
map (endpapers)
Numbers in **bold** refer to the
illustrations

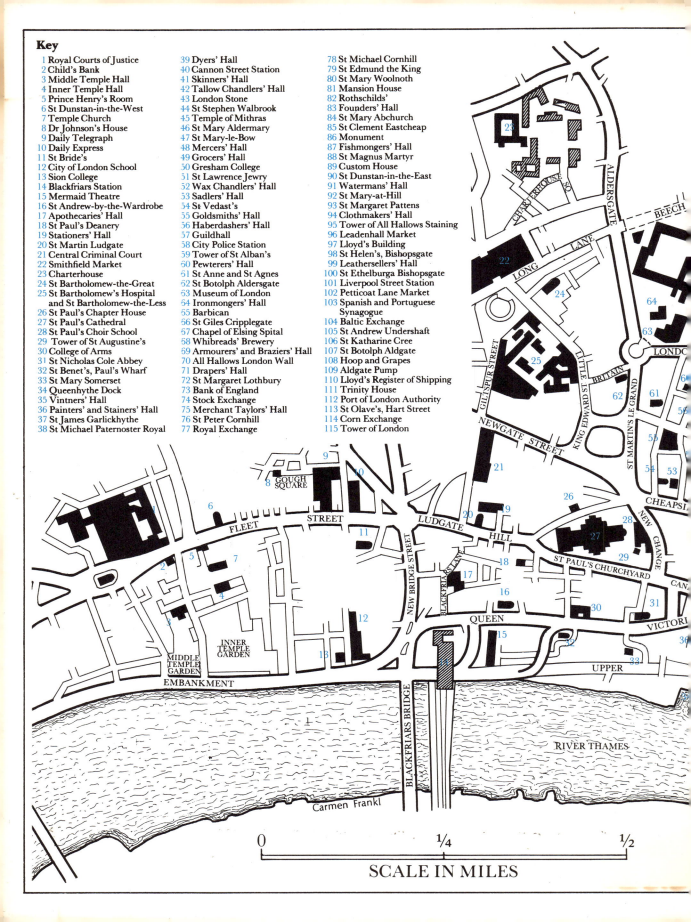

Key

1 Royal Courts of Justice
2 Child's Bank
3 Middle Temple Hall
4 Inner Temple Hall
5 Prince Henry's Room
6 St Dunstan-in-the-West
7 Temple Church
8 Dr Johnson's House
9 Daily Telegraph
10 Daily Express
11 St Bride's
12 City of London School
13 Sion College
14 Blackfriars Station
15 Mermaid Theatre
16 St Andrew-by-the-Wardrobe
17 Apothecaries' Hall
18 St Paul's Deanery
19 Stationers' Hall
20 St Martin Ludgate
21 Central Criminal Court
22 Smithfield Market
23 Charterhouse
24 St Bartholomew-the-Great
25 St Bartholomew's Hospital
   and St Bartholomew-the-Less
26 St Paul's Chapter House
27 St Paul's Cathedral
28 St Paul's Choir School
29 Tower of St Augustine's
30 College of Arms
31 St Nicholas Cole Abbey
32 St Benet's, Paul's Wharf
33 St Mary Somerset
34 Queenhythe Dock
35 Vintners' Hall
36 Painters' and Stainers' Hall
37 St James Garlickhythe
38 St Michael Paternoster Royal

39 Dyers' Hall
40 Cannon Street Station
41 Skinners' Hall
42 Tallow Chandlers' Hall
43 London Stone
44 St Stephen Walbrook
45 Temple of Mithras
46 St Mary Aldermary
47 St Mary-le-Bow
48 Mercers' Hall
49 Grocers' Hall
50 Gresham College
51 St Lawrence Jewry
52 Wax Chandlers' Hall
53 Sadlers' Hall
54 St Vedast's
55 Goldsmiths' Hall
56 Haberdashers' Hall
57 Guildhall
58 City Police Station
59 Tower of St Alban's
50 Pewterers' Hall
61 St Anne and St Agnes
62 St Botolph Aldersgate
63 Museum of London
64 Ironmongers' Hall
65 Barbican
66 St Giles Cripplegate
67 Chapel of Elsing Spital
68 Whibreads' Brewery
69 Armourers' and Braziers' Hall
70 All Hallows London Wall
71 Drapers' Hall
72 St Margaret Lothbury
73 Bank of England
74 Stock Exchange
75 Merchant Taylors' Hall
76 St Peter Cornhill
77 Royal Exchange

78 St Michael Cornhill
79 St Edmund the King
80 St Mary Woolnoth
81 Mansion House
82 Rothschilds'
83 Founders' Hall
84 St Mary Abchurch
85 St Clement Eastcheap
86 Monument
87 Fishmongers' Hall
88 St Magnus Martyr
89 Custom House
90 St Dunstan-in-the-East
91 Watermans' Hall
92 St Mary-at-Hill
93 St Margaret Pattens
94 Clothmakers' Hall
95 Tower of All Hallows Staining
96 Leadenhall Market
97 Lloyd's Building
98 St Helen's, Bishopsgate
99 Leathersellers' Hall
100 St Ethelburga Bishopsgate
101 Liverpool Street Station
102 Petticoat Lane Market
103 Spanish and Portuguese
    Synagogue
104 Baltic Exchange
105 St Andrew Undershaft
106 St Katharine Cree
107 St Botolph Aldgate
108 Hoop and Grapes
109 Aldgate Pump
110 Lloyd's Register of Shipping
111 Trinity House
112 Port of London Authority
113 St Olave's, Hart Street
114 Corn Exchange
115 Tower of London

SCALE IN MILES

0   1/4   1/2